P9-EMF-321

The United States and Saudi Arabia: Ambivalent Allies

Also of Interest

The Foreign Policies of Arab States, Bahgat Korany and Ali E. Hillal Dessouki

Religion and State in the Kingdom of Saudi Arabia, Ayman Al-Yassini

The Gulf and the Search for Strategic Stability: Saudi Arabia, the Military Balance in the Gulf, and Trends in the Arab-Israeli Military Balance, Anthony H. Cordesman

Political Adaptation in Sa'udi Arabia, Summer Scott Huyette

†*Security in the Middle East,* edited by Samuel F. Wells, Jr., and Mark A. Bruzonsky

The Middle East Military Balance 1984, Mark A. Heller, Dov Tamari, and Zeev Eytan

The Arab World: An International Statistical Directory, Rodney Wilson

Local Politics and Development in the Middle East, edited by Louis J. Cantori and Iliya Harik

Middle East Politics: The Military Dimension, J. C. Hurewitz

†*The Government and Politics of the Middle East and North Africa,* edited by David E. Long and Bernard Reich

†*Political Behavior in the Arab States,* Tawfic E. Farah

Economic Diplomacy: The Political Dynamics of Oil Leverage, M. S. Daoudi and M. S. Dajani

OPEC, the Gulf, and the World Petroleum Market: A Study in Government Policy and Downstream Operations, Fereidun Fesharaki and David T. Isaak

Oil Strategy and Politics, 1941–1981, Walter J. Levy (edited by Melvin A. Conant)

†*Islam: Continuity and Change in the Modern World,* John Obert Voll

†Available in hardcover and paperback.

About the Book and Author

The United States and Saudi Arabia: Ambivalent Allies
David E. Long

U.S.-Saudi relations have been marked by ambivalence since their inception over 50 years ago. The Arab-Israeli conflict, the division between buyer and seller of oil, the superpower–small state dichotomy, and the divergence of cultures, traditions, and perceptions have all contributed to the anomalies that have marked the relationship between the two countries, although mutual interest has, over time, outweighed mutual antagonism. Dr. Long examines the major factors affecting their association—economic, commercial, military, and political as well as oil-related factors—and develops the thesis that each has evolved a unique internal dynamic and an existence independent of the others. It is primarily in times of crisis that the factors have overlapped in the minds of decision makers, Saudi and American alike. The author argues that a knowledge of the development of each individual element is crucial for understanding the intricacies of current U.S.-Saudi relations.

David E. Long is serving on the Secretary of State's Policy Planning Staff. He prepared this book while a senior fellow at the Middle East Research Institute, University of Pennsylvania. He is the author of *The Persian Gulf: An Introduction to Its Peoples, Politics, and Economics* (Westview, revised edition 1978), and coeditor of *The Government and Politics of the Middle East and North Africa* (Westview, 1980).

Published in cooperation with the
Middle East Research Institute,
University of Pennsylvania

The United States and Saudi Arabia: Ambivalent Allies

David E. Long

Westview Press / Boulder and London

MERI Special Studies, Number 3

This book was prepared while the author was a Senior Fellow at MERI, 1982-1983.

Published in 1985 in the United States of America by Westview Press, Inc., 5500 Central Avenue, Boulder, Colorado 80301; Frederick A. Praeger, Publisher

Library of Congress Cataloging in Publication Data
Long, David E.
The United States and Saudi Arabia.
(MERI special studies series; no. 3)
Published in cooperation with the Middle East Research Institute, University of Pennsylvania.
Bibliography: p.
Includes index.
1. United States—Foreign relations—Saudi Arabia.
2. Saudi Arabia—Foreign relations—United States.
3. United States—Foreign relations—1945- .
I. Title. II. Series.
E183.8.S25L66 1985 327.73053′8 85-3270
ISBN 0-8133-0208-0

Printed and bound in the United States of America

10 9 8 7 6 5 4 3 2 1

This book is dedicated to all the men and women
of the United States and Saudi Arabia
who have served their countries
in the promotion of better U.S.-Saudi relations.

Contents

Preface

Communicating to a Western reader the nature of U.S. relations with a non-Western country is an awesome task. Understanding the issues is only part of the problem. The perceptions of those issues by citizens of the two nations are often, if not always, very different, and for a Westerner to attempt to understand—much less communicate—Saudi perceptions is little short of presumptuous. For example, there is a tendency, when analyzing Saudis' political behavior, implicitly to ascribe to them a Western mentality. Although this may not detract from understanding the issues, it does detract from understanding how Saudis view those issues, and hence why they did what they did or what they might do in the future. Thus, even though this is not a study of U.S.-Saudi political behavior (with a capital B), an attempt has been made to take account of behavioral factors implicit in the relationship.

An even more formidable problem is that of scope. In the totality of U.S.-Saudi relations, the major and positive role of private U.S. companies, particularly Aramco, is virtually unique; the person-to-person relationships of private Americans in Saudi Arabia and of Saudis in the United States, principally in colleges and universities, have also been important. Given the paucity of research on official relations, however, and their key importance in understanding the nature and direction of the overall relationship, I thought it more useful to leave U.S. private-sector relations with Saudi Arabia to others and to limit the scope of this study to government-to-government relations.

A final conceptual problem involves the methodological approach to the subject. I settled on a historical approach because although the continuities of U.S.-Saudi relations are not well known, they are central to understanding the nature and direction of current and ongoing relations. All too often, policy debate in the United States over U.S.-Saudi relations has been severely restricted by this lack of a historical dimension. For example, the congressional debates over the U.S. sale of F-15 aircraft to Saudi Arabia in 1978 and AWACS aircraft in 1982 paid scant attention to historical developments. Both sales can be linked directly to a U.S. promise made in 1963 to conduct an air defense survey for Saudi Arabia if King Faysal would agree to a settlement with Egypt's President Nasser over the Yemeni Civil War. The agreement was stillborn, but the survey was duly made, and from it came the long series of largely U.S.-recommended efforts to improve Saudi air defenses that ultimately led to the purchase of F-15s and AWACS. The level and rate of development toward those systems was known, at least in a general way, years before the sales were ever made.

No endeavor such as this book can be successful without the generous aid and support of many people. I am particularly grateful to Tom Naff, the director of the Middle East Research Institute at the University of Pennsylvania, for providing me with a stimulating and congenial atmosphere in which to do the basic research during 1982 and 1983. I must also thank the Carthage Foundation and the Shell Foundation for their generous support of the project.

Numerous friends and colleagues in government, academia, and the private sector provided excellent advice, suggestions, and comments. I would like especially to thank Ron Neumann, in charge of Saudi affairs in the State Department, as well as Ambassadors Hermann Eilts, Nicholas Thacher, Talcott Seelye, and John West, who read the manuscript in its entirety and provided me with invaluable commentary. Finally, I should like to thank Magida Abboud of the Middle East Research Institute, who performed the odious task of typing the manuscript, and my wife, Barbara, who put up with me during the trying time of research.

David E. Long
Burke, Virginia

The United States and Saudi Arabia: Ambivalent Allies

1
Introduction: Constant Interests Among Changing Perceptions

Relations between the United States and the Kingdom of Saudi Arabia have existed for roughly a half-century. During most of that time, Saudi Arabia has been treated by the West with all but total neglect. Whatever interest existed was generated by the oil companies, an occasional stray diplomat or two, and military planners who were worried less about the country itself than about the enemy hands into which it could fall. Even Western academic interest in the Middle East largely ignored Saudi Arabia. In a 1977 survey of scholarly literature of the region, only 6 of 120 books and 19 of 5,500 articles surveyed mentioned the Kingdom.[1]

The Arab-Israeli war of 1973 and subsequent Arab oil embargo changed all that. Suddenly, Saudi Arabia found itself in the glare of an international spotlight focusing on oil. New terms such as "petrodollars," "petropower," and "the oil weapon" came into vogue not only in the popular media but also in technical, government, and academic jargon. By that strange process that occasionally causes elements of international relations to appear all out of proportion, Saudi Arabia quickly acquired some of the trappings of a semisuperpower, at least in the areas of international oil and finance. Several years passed before a proper sense of proportion returned. Although one can now view Saudi Arabia with more equanimity than one could in the mid-1970s, the international spotlight on the Kingdom in the post-1973 period has made objective analysis of U.S.-Saudi relations as difficult as did the obscurity of the pre-1973 period.

U.S. Perceptions of Saudi Arabia

The radically changing environment within which U.S.-Saudi relations have been conducted over the years has resulted in changing perceptions in the United States of the nature and priority of its interests with

Saudi Arabia. In the 1930s, whatever perception of Saudi Arabia was held at all in the United States was limited to a few oil men and an even smaller number of government officials interested in insuring against trade inequities for U.S. firms doing business overseas.

In the 1940s, official U.S. interest in Saudi Arabia abruptly increased with the outbreak of World War II. Both Saudi Arabia's newly discovered oil resources and its strategic location on the flank of the Near Eastern theater of military operations made the Kingdom of major importance to the United States in the context of the war. This importance began to wane at the end of the war but was quickly revived by the cold war and the direct Soviet threat to the entire Middle East in the postwar years.

The establishment of Israel in 1948 created a major political obstruction to U.S.-Saudi relations. Nevertheless, throughout the 1950s and 1960s, Saudi Arabia's role in the Arab-Israeli problem received less priority in Washington than the strategic military threat to the Kingdom emanating from the cold war. In the 1960s, superpower politics entered a period of détente, but in the Middle East the rise of militant Arab nationalism, which professed a closer affinity to the socialism of the Soviet bloc than to the capitalism of the West, was a major factor in preventing détente from spreading to the region.

In 1973, U.S. priorities again underwent a change. Not only had Saudi Arabia become the world's principal oil exporter, but the United States had also become a net importer of oil, dependent on Middle East oil for the first time. Moreover, as the terms of trade shifted from a buyers' market to a sellers' market, the oil-exporting countries took from the oil companies the function of setting prices and production rates. On the political side, the Kingdom, which for years had remained steadfastly on the back bench of intra-Arab politics, suddenly took over the leadership of the Arab moderates and almost single-handedly imposed the Arab oil embargo of 1973-1974.

This turn of events produced a great ambivalence in U.S. perceptions of Saudi Arabia. On the one hand, as leader of the resurgent moderate Arab states, so long placed on the defensive by Arab radicals, Saudi Arabia was seen as a strong friend and a vital link in winning the Arabs over to terms that could result in a comprehensive Arab-Israeli peace. On the other hand, the energy shortage of 1974-1975, largely induced by price hikes decreed by the Organization of Petroleum Exporting Countries (OPEC) and the Saudi-led Arab oil embargo, created the image of Saudis as sinister oil shaykhs. This negative image was fostered by Israel and its supporters. They appeared to realize, probably before the Saudis themselves did, that Saudi oil power had the potential to threaten Israel in a way that the combined military power of the

Arabs could not, by presenting the United States with difficult choices between its political commitment to Israel and its strategic interest in Arab oil.

In the meantime, the Soviet strategic threat again intensified in the aftermath of the fall of the shah of Iran in 1978 and the Soviet invasion of Afghanistan the following year. Despite the renewed emphasis on strategic concerns, U.S. perceptions of Saudi Arabia remained ambivalent. Proponents of strong U.S.-Saudi relations argued for stronger defense ties lest the Kingdom go the way of Iran. Critics warned against such ties on grounds that the Kingdom was so unstable that it would probably collapse of its own weight, leaving the United States holding the bag.

Saudi Perceptions of the United States

In contrast to changing U.S. perceptions of Saudi Arabia, Saudi perceptions of the United States have remained relatively constant over the years. This stems in good measure from the Saudi view of the world in general, a view substantially different in many respects from that of other Arab countries. Two apparently contradictory themes are paramount in Saudi perceptions of the world: an extraordinary cultural self-assurance based on a strong sense of self-identity and a heightened sense of insecurity based on the historical experience of being surrounded by enemies.

The similarities of Saudis and the Arabs to the north and west of them—they share a common language and an Islamic religious and cultural heritage—are so pronounced that for many Western observers, and indeed for many Arabs, the differences are somewhat obscured. Yet, it is the differences—as much as if not more than the similarities—that provide the key to understanding the uniquely Saudi world view and hence to understanding Saudi foreign policy behavior generally and toward the United States in particular. These differences can be divided into three areas: perceptions of Pan-Arabism, perceptions of Western imperialism, and perceptions of Pan-Islamism.[2]

For much of the Arab world, Pan-Arabism is a comparatively recent phenomenon. Its rapid rise was to a great extent a reaction to the rise of nineteenth-century Western secular nationalism and to the abrupt penetration of Western ideas and scholarship into the region. At the same time, U.S. Presbyterian missionaries in what is now Lebanon had as much to do with the rise of modern Arab nationalism as anyone by virtue of their reintroducing many of the Arab classics in Arabic on their own presses. Recognition of the recent nature of Pan-Arabism is embodied in the political parties of Syria and Iraq, the Socialist Arab Ba'th party. *Ba'th* in Arabic means *renaissance* or *rebirth.*

The head-on collision of Western imperialism and traditional Arab society, beginning with Napoleon's invasion of Egypt in 1798, was another major determinant in the development of Arab nationalism and of contemporary Arab perceptions of the world. For more than 150 years, most of the Arab world was under the influence, if not the direct control, of the European powers.

From this legacy, many positive elements developed. Foreign domination, however, also created frustration, xenophobia, and bitterness, all focused on Western imperialism. Much of the politics of Arab nationalism was thus the politics of dissent. The espousal of Western secular socialist ideologies by most militant Arab nationalists is a case in point. Socialism, insofar as it is a Western, secular ideology, is antithetical to Islamic economic theory. This is not to say that many Western concepts of social welfare are not also found in Islam. Yet, to militant Arab nationalists, who equated capitalism with perceived social and economic inequities suffered under European domination, socialism served both as an ideological avenue to social, political, and economic equality and as an antidote to imperialism. That its appeal was more emotional than theoretical can be seen in the conflicting policies and programs implemented by Arab governments all in the name of socialism.

Another product of the impact of Western imperialism on traditional Middle Eastern society was the rise of Pan-Islamism, particularly in the late nineteenth and early twentieth centuries. Insulated and isolated for centuries, Islamic society suddenly had to cope with an environment that did not seem to coincide with classical Islam. In reaction to Western imperialism, the Pan-Islamic movement to a great extent arose as an attempt to revitalize the Muslim world, spiritually and otherwise, and to enable it to withstand alien ideas and ideologies.

The Saudi experience with all three of these perceptions—Arabism, Islamism, and Western imperialism—was very different from that of most other Arab states. The ruling elite of the country is from Najd, as central Arabia is called. Central Arabia—the political and spiritual, as well as geographical, heartland of Saudi Arabia—is considered by Najdis to be the heartland of Arabism as well. Unlike Arabs outside the Arabian Peninsula, central Arabians never lost their sense of Arab identity and consequently never felt the need to rediscover it. Najdi Arabian identity is primarily based not on historical, linguistic, cultural, or even religious heritage, important as those factors are, but rather on blood. Virtually everyone can trace his family ancestry as far back as history and his tribal ties beyond that. The assurance of knowing their identity has given most Saudis a self-confidence almost unmatched in the Middle East, particularly outside the Arabian Peninsula. Identity crises, so common among Western-educated elites from traditional societies, are rare indeed in Saudi Arabia.

Perceptions of the Islamic world are also different in Saudi Arabia. Whereas the revival of Pan-Islam took place in the rest of the Muslim world largely in the nineteenth and twentieth centuries, and to a great extent in reaction to Western secular ideas, Saudi Arabia's Islamic revival took place in the eighteenth century with little or no reference to the West. In 1744-1745, Muhammad bin Saud (c. A.D. 1703-1704 to 1792), amir of the small Najdi town of Dir'iyyah and founder of the Al Saud dynasty, came under the influence of a native religious revivalist, Muhammad bin Abd al-Wahhab. The latter had come to Dir'iyyah after he had been driven out of the nearby town of Uyainah for his religious beliefs. Abd al-Wahhab's revival, subseuqently called Wahhabism after its founder,[3] was drawn from the writings of an early Islamic jurist, Ibn Taymiyyah (c. A.D. 1262 to 1328), who followed the Hanbali school of jurisprudence, the most conservative of the four recognized schools of Sunni Islam. Muhammad bin Saud became the patron of the revival movement, which from that day to this has served as the ideological base for legitimizing Saudi rule.

In the 1920s, when Abd al-Aziz (known in the West as Ibn Saud) was consolidating modern Saudi Arabia, he occupied the Hijaz with its holy cities of Makkah and al-Madina. As guardians of these two holiest sites in Islam, Saudis perceive of themselves as having added responsibility as defenders of the Islamic way of life throughout the Muslim world.

Saudis have had a very different experience with Western imperialism from most of their Arab brothers in that they have never been subjected to European colonial domination. Thus they never developed the inferiority complex toward the West displayed by other Arabs under European political domination, nor did they develop the same degree of frustration and anti-Western xenophobia. For most Saudis, imperialism is seen in terms of a threat to the Islamic world and its Islamic way of life. Their perceptions of the value of relations with the United States are thus far less influenced by the psychological baggage of antiimperialism than are the perceptions of many other Arabs.

Because Western influences were less pronounced in Saudi Arabia than in most of the Middle East until quite recently, the classical Islamic view of international relations has remained more intact. This view basically envisions a bipolar world, made up of the *Dar al-Islam* (territory under Islamic, or God's, Law) and the *Dar al-Harb* (territory of war, that is, outside the rule of law). Within Dar al-Islam are not only Muslims, but all monotheists subscribing to a divinely inspired revelation.

Called *Ahl al-Kitab,* the "People of the Book," they include Christians and Jews.

One can quickly see how easy it would be to adapt the present-day bipolar world to the classical Islamic bipolar world. It need not even be done consciously. Dar al-Islam becomes the free world and Dar al-Harb becomes the Communist world, opposed less for its political and economic doctrines than for its essentially secular, atheistic nature.

In light of this perception, one can also more easily understand Saudi foreign policy priorities. For example, dividing the world into North and South, as much of the Third World does, is not a high priority in the Saudi scheme of things. Far more important is the preservation of monotheism against atheist, secular ideologies. This explains Saudi antipathy to Marxism and to secular, radical Arab nationalism and also explains why Saudi foreign aid to the Third World follows a well-defined order of priority. Arab states are accorded first priority, followed by non-Arab Muslim states, and finally by non-Arab, non-Muslim states facing an internal or external Communist threat.

In cooperating with the United States, the Saudis see themselves not as "agents of imperialism," but as fellow monotheists facing a global, atheistic, Marxist threat. The Saudis would no doubt greatly prefer to be the senior partner in defending the free world, a role classical Islam reserves for Muslims alone. Under the circumstances of Western technological superiority, however, such a proposition is simply out of the question. Thus, Saudi perceptions of the world have had such strength and depth as to hold constant the Saudi perceptions of the need for close relations with the United States.

There are, of course, many inconsistencies in adopting the classical Islamic theory of international relations to the contemporary bipolar world, just as there are many inconsistencies in contemporary Western perceptions of bipolarity. Far too many U.S. foreign-policy makers have attempted to force all international problems into the bipolar mold of U.S.-Soviet rivalry whether they fit the mold or not. By the same token, many aspects of the international system do not fit the Saudi bipolar mold either. The most difficult anomaly for them involves the Arab-Israeli problem. Israelis, as Jews, are to be respected as People of the Book. Yet Zionism, in the Saudi view, has not only unjustly deprived Arabs of their basic territorial rights of self-determination but has also, since 1967, usurped control of the third holiest site in Sunni Islam after Makkah and al-Madina—al-Aqsa in Jerusalem. Moreover, the prolongation of the problem threatens the entire Arab world by radicalizing its youth, bitter and frustrated over continued Israeli occupation and creeping annexation of the remaining Arab territories of pre-1948 Palestine.

Intellectually, the Saudis have resolved this dilemma by distinguishing between Judaism, a revered religion, and Zionism, an alien, secular, political doctrine. It has become more difficult for the Saudis to rationalize their relations with the United States in terms of the Arab-Israeli problem, however. On the one hand, the United States is seen as the ultimate defense against world domination by communism; on the other hand, it is the ultimate supporter of Zionism. This paradox has been the principal reason for the high degree of ambivalence in Saudi Arabia's relations with the United States since 1948.

At this point, a word of caution is in order regarding how strictly to hold the Saudis to their perceptions of the international system. For the most part, Saudis are no different from any other people in that they are seldom introspective, nor do they consciously or consistently apply psychological or ideological formulas to everyday, foreign-policy decision making. Their perceptions of the world, while widespread, are by no means highly refined into those intellectual models that Western political scientists so love to employ. Moreover, Saudis—as well as most non-Western societies—tend to have a higher tolerance for inconsistency than Western societies, so that conceptual paradoxes bother them much less than they might Western scholars studying Saudi foreign policy behavior.

A second major perceptual ingredient in the Saudi view of the world that influences its relations with the United States is a very highly developed "encirclement syndrome." As is often the case among insular societies, Najdis, surrounded by a sea of sand, have developed over time a perception of constantly being surrounded by enemies. Historically, this perception is not all that far off the mark. During the eighteenth and nineteenth centuries, the Ottomans, from their possessions in the Hijaz on the Red Sea and al-Hasa Oasis near the Gulf, constantly harassed Najd; in 1818, an Ottoman-Egyptian force actually invaded central Arabia and destroyed the Saudi capital at Dir'iyyah. When the force departed four years later, the Sauds rebuilt their capital at Riyadh, a short distance away, but the ruins of Dir'iyyah can still be viewed as a reminder of foreign invasion.

In the late nineteenth century, Najd was overrun by the Al Rashids of northern Arabia, who drove the Sauds from Riyadh just before the turn of the century. It was Abd al-Aziz's recapture of Riyadh in 1902 that started him on the road toward the restoration of Saudi rule and the creation of modern Saudi Arabia. In the 1920s, Abd al-Aziz drove the Hashimite King Husayn (Hussein) from the Hijaz; two of Husayn's sons were made rulers of neighboring Iraq and Transjordan (renamed Jordan in 1948) by the British and were seen as threats right up to the late 1950s. By that time, Egypt's President Jamal Abd al-Nasser and his brand of Arab socialism threatened to inundate the entire Arab world, helping to create a Saudi-Hashimite rapprochement.

The feeling of encirclement remained particularly strong against Nasser in the 1960s as a result of his support for the republican regime in Yemen during the eight-year-long Yemeni Civil War. The Saudis opposed the Yemeni republicans during the civil war until a Saudi reconciliation with the republican regime was effected in 1970.

The Saudi sense of encirclement has been no less strong in the 1970s and 1980s. The British departure from Aden in 1967 was followed by the establishment of a Marxist regime in South Yemen. Under Soviet patronage, South Yemen has had several armed clashes with the Saudis and has supported Marxist insurgencies in North Yemen and in the neighboring Dhufar province of Oman. To the southwest, the Soviets have consolidated their position in Ethiopía under a Marxist regime, and to the east they are involved in a military attempt to subdue Afghanistan. To the north, radical regimes in Damascus and Baghdad, though currently on relatively good terms with Riyadh, are always a potential threat. Even more threatening at present, however, is the mercurial, antagonistic regime in Iran, waging a devastating war with Iraq that has shown little sign of abating. The Iranians have made it clear that after Iraq, the Saudi regime leads the list of governments they wish to see overthrown. And finally, there is Israel, in the northwest, whose antagonism toward Saudi Arabia has so greatly increased following the 1973 Arab-Israeli war and the Arab oil embargo. Israel's hostile intentions toward all Arabs, in the Saudi view, were unmistakably laid bare in the invasion of Lebanon in the summer of 1982.

The deep-seated sense of encirclement has further reinforced the Saudi feeling of insecurity in the face of the various internal and external threats with which the Kingdom has had to deal over the years. The resulting search for security has been a major element in Saudi relations with the United States. At the same time, the insecurity bred of an encirclement syndrome stands in sharp contrast to the self-confidence bred of a strong sense of self-identity. It is an anomaly that further contributes to the ambivalence with which Saudis have long approached their relations with the United States.

A Stable Community of Interests

Despite changing perceptions and conditions, the basic common interests—and differences—of U.S.-Saudi relations have remained constant over the last fifty years. The following chapters will examine the development and significance of U.S.-Saudi ties in the spheres of oil, military, economic-commercial, and political affairs. Important events in each of these spheres have obviously had an impact on the others. Yet each sphere has had sufficiently independent characteristics and has developed sufficiently independent dynamics to warrant its being examined separately.

Notes

1. See Ralph Braibanti and Fouad Abdul-Salam Al-Farsy, "Saudi Arabia: A Developmental Perspective," in *Journal of South Asian and Middle Eastern Studies* 1, no. 2 (September 1977), pp. 3–34.

2. For a more detailed discussion of Saudi perceptions of the world, see David E. Long, "King Faisal's World View," in Willard A. Beling, ed., *King Faisal and the Modernisation of Saudi Arabia* (London: Croom Helm; and Boulder, Colo.: Westview Press; 1980).

3. Followers of the revival usually do not use the term "Wahhabi," which to them implies worship of a human being. Strict monotheists, they prefer the term "Muwahhidin," or "Unitarians."

2
U.S.-Saudi Oil Relations

The Evolution of U.S. Interests in Middle East Oil: 1919–1933

Oil has been a basic factor in U.S.-Saudi relations from the beginning. In fact, earliest official U.S. interest in Middle East oil occurred during World War I. Prior to the war, there was little public incentive to encourage exploration for foreign sources, since the United States was already the world's leading producer, and its own reserves appeared more than adequate for domestic needs. As the Allies became cut off from their own foreign sources during the war, however, and the United States became the main supplier of oil for the Allied war effort, official U.S. interest in overseas supplies increased. Concern for secure reserves persisted after the war, despite a major expansion in domestic production. The chief geologist for the U.S. Geological Survey expressed this concern in May 1919 when he urged U.S. oil companies to move "more aggressively into South America and the Middle East."[1]

During the 1920s, official U.S. interest in Middle East oil remained high, but the focus shifted from strategic military concerns to insuring that U.S. oil companies would not be frozen out of concessions in the region by the British and French. One cause for concern was the San Remo Agreement of April 24, 1920. In that agreement, Britain attempted to secure French support for British control of the Mosul oil concession—claimed by the old British-dominated Turkish Petroleum Company (TPC)—by granting to the French the 25 percent share in TPC that had formerly been owned by German interests. The Treaty of Severes of August 10, 1920, confirmed the transfer of the Mosul oil fields from Turkish sovereignty to what was to become the British-controlled mandate of Iraq, and TPC, renamed the Iraq Petroleum Company (IPC), retained the concession.

The creation of TPC had resulted largely from efforts of an Armenian entrepreneur, Calouste Gulbenkian, who in 1914 had drawn up an agreement for 50 percent ownership by British interests and 25 percent ownership each by Dutch and German interests. Gulbenkian was awarded a 5 percent beneficiary, nonvoting interest (2.5 percent from the Dutch and 2.5 percent from the British). The agreement included a clause eliminating competition among TPC owners in developing Middle East oil resources. This self-denial clause, the precursor of the so-called Red Line Agreement of 1928, was included in order to prevent cutthroat competition among the concessionaires.[2]

Taken together, the British-French-Dutch monopoly and the self-denial clause appeared to the U.S. State Department to be contrary to the "open-door" policy for commercial access to the mandated territories that the United States was pursuing.[3] The United States mounted pressure on Britain to allow U.S. oil companies full access to the British mandates in the Middle East, particularly Iraq, and went so far as to challenge the legal validity of the TPC claim. It was clear, however, that the State Department was more interested in U.S. participation than in the legal validity of the claim, for the United States proposed to Britain that the claims be arbitrated, provided any agreement worked out would recognize the right of U.S. firms to operate in the mandated territories without prejudice or discrimination.[4]

In the meantime, with State Department encouragement, seven U.S. oil companies—Standard Oil of New Jersey (now Exxon), Standard Oil of New York (now Mobil), Gulf Oil Corporation, the Texas Company (Texaco), Sinclair, Atlantic Oil Company (now part of Atlantic-Richfield, or ARCO), and Pan American Petroleum (Standard Oil of Indiana)—created a joint venture known as the Near East Development Corporation. With U.S. government backing, this group received 23.75 percent equity in IPC in July 1928. (Sinclair and Texaco had in the meantime dropped out, and the shares of Pan American and Atlantic had been purchased by Standard of New Jersey and Standard of New York.)[5] As a precondition to participation in IPC, however, the U.S. group agreed to abide by the self-denial clause by signing what became known as the Red Line Agreement. The State Department gave its blessing to these proceedings even though they flew in the face of the open-door principles it had been so stoutly defending. This reaction was an indication of the pragmatism with which the United States approached the entire issue.

In September 1928, the chief executive officers of the Anglo-Persian Oil Company (half owner of IPC and subsequently renamed British Petroleum), Royal Dutch Shell, Gulf Oil Corporation, and Standard Oil of New Jersey met at Achnacarry Castle in Scotland and agreed upon a formula for market allocations in order to prevent what was then an oil glut from causing the entire world oil market to collapse. The As Is Agreement, as it came to be called, limited market shares, and the Red Line Agreement limited exploration activities. Together, they were to determine the course of international oil transactions until World

War II. Indeed, until the 1970s, control over production rates and prices rested firmly in the hands of the major international oil companies.[6]

Official U.S. Interests and the Saudi Arabian Concession: 1933–1940

Official U.S. interest in Middle East oil continued in the late 1920s and early 1930s in Kuwait and Bahrain. This interest was in large measure a continuation of earlier U.S. government interests in insuring participation by U.S. oil companies in the exploitation of Middle East oil. A marked decline in official U.S. involvement in Middle East oil in the 1930s resulted partly from the success in insuring U.S. participation and partly from the lessening strategic interest in oil itself. As oil production grew during the interwar period, and as world demand fell as a result of the Great Depression, a worldwide oil glut developed. Ironically, it was in this period of minimal official U.S. involvement that U.S. oil companies became established in Saudi Arabia. It could even be argued that lack of official support helped the companies' chances more than it hurt.

The Americans were not the first to be interested in Saudi oil. In 1923, Major Frank Holmes, an entrepreneur and adventurer from New Zealand, obtained a concession to explore for oil from Abd al-Aziz (Ibn Saud), then sultan of Najd. Holmes was aided in obtaining the concession by a Lebanese American, Ameen Rihani, who had become a confidant of the sultan. Abd al-Aziz did not wish to open his country to the foreign political exploitation that he had seen follow in the wake of foreign oil concessions in neighboring countries, nor did he really believe that Holmes's Eastern and General Syndicate would find oil. This latter view was shared by many in the oil industry who did not believe that Saudi geology was favorable for the discovery of oil.[7] Nevertheless, Abd al-Aziz was then constantly in need of money and saw the concession as a relatively low-risk means of acquiring some.

Holmes, on the other hand, was never really interested in finding oil, but rather in selling the concession to an oil company that was. In this he had no success, and in 1928 the concession lapsed. In the meantime, Holmes had also obtained a concession in Bahrain, an island amirate 23 miles off the Arabian coast. Gulf Oil Corporation picked up this concession, but was unable to pursue it because of the Red Line Agreement and subsequently sold it to Standard Oil Company of California (Socal), which was not a signatory to the agreement. Bahrain had a treaty with Britain forbidding oil exploration in the amirate by a non-British company; to get around this restriction, Socal simply created a Canadian subsidiary, the Bahrain Petroleum Company (Bapco).

In May 1932, Bapco struck oil. In this endeavor it had full U.S. government backing.

Buoyed by the discovery in Bahrain, Socal geologists revived interest in Saudi Arabia. With the help of H. St. John B. Philby, an Englishman who had met Abd al-Aziz while on an official British mission during World War I and had stayed on to become a close advisor, and of Karl Twitchell, an American who had previously surveyed Saudi water and mineral resources, Socal persuaded King Abd al-Aziz (he had become king of the Hijaz in 1926 and king of Saudi Arabia in 1932) to grant a concession in May 1933. It was officially ratified by royal decree in July.

Abd al-Aziz had had a change of heart about granting oil concessions since his experience with Holmes and was now actively seeking one. With the growing world depression in the 1930s and the increase of international tensions leading to World War II, the number of Hajjis, or pilgrims to Maccah, had begun to decline. As Hajj receipts were the principal source of income for Saudi Arabia, the Kingdom's always fragile financial state was rapidly becoming more precarious than ever.[8] Abd al-Aziz entertained offers not only from Socal, but from IPC as well. Socal's success can probably be attributed both to its more attractive financial terms (including a £50,000 advance against future royalties) and to the Saudi view that Americans were solely interested in commercial dealings and not in exerting political influence or in entertaining political designs.[9]

Socal assigned the concession to its wholly owned subsidiary, California Arabian Standard Oil Company (Casoc), in November 1933. The previous September the first oil prospectors had stepped ashore at the small Gulf village of Jubayl, present site of Saudi Arabia's ambitious petrochemical center and naval base. On April 30, 1935, drilling commenced on Dammam Well No. 1, at the same depth that had been successful in Bahrain. It and the next five wells proved disappointing, however, with insufficient flow for commercial purposes. Dammam No. 7 was spudded in on December 7, 1936, and drilling continued beneath the Bahrain zone. On March 3, 1938, Dammam No. 7 began producing over fifteen hundred barrels per day (b/d) and has been producing ever since. Saudi Arabia had entered the oil age.

In the meantime, the international oil glut had caused anxieties to rise throughout the oil industry about the impact on the market of Saudi and Bahraini oil coming on stream. Negotiators between Socal and other major companies were making little progress, but at that juncture a temporary solution was inadvertently found. Texaco had developed extensive overseas markets but had virtually no overseas sources, whereas Socal had overseas sources but few markets. In 1936, the two companies combined their overseas interests in the Near East and Asia, placing Bapco and Casoc under a jointly owned subsidiary, the California Texas Oil Company Ltd., or Caltex. Texaco purchased half interest in Casoc for $3 million plus $18 million in deferred equity. Concern over entry of Caltex on the world oil market continued even after 1936, and there were sporadic efforts to obtain IPC equity in the Saudi concession. All of these efforts were overtaken by the events accompanying the outbreak of World War II, however. (On January 31, 1944, Casoc's name was changed to the Arabian American Oil Company—Aramco.)

U.S. Wartime Interests: 1940–1947

With the coming of World War II, official U.S. interest was rekindled not only in Saudi Arabia's oil but in the strategic location of the country. Initial interest was sparked by the growing financial crisis confronting King Abd al-Aziz as Hajj receipts continued to fall on the eve of the war. By early 1941, Casoc, which had been more or less keeping the Saudi treasury afloat with loans and advances on future royalties, felt that the situation was getting out of hand. The company turned to the U.S. government to help bail Abd al-Aziz out of his difficulties. The result of this *démarche* was some long and drawn-out negotiations within the U.S. government and among the United States, Britain, and Saudi Arabia before financial aid was finally forthcoming in February 1943.

The question of aid had broad commercial, financial, and strategic implications. The narrower oil ramifications involved insuring strategic oil reserves for the United States. In June 1943, Interior Secretary Harold Ickes wrote President Franklin D. Roosevelt recommending that the secretary of commerce be given the authority to "acquire and participate in the development of foreign oil reserves" through a publicly owned corporation to be managed by a board of directors that included the secretaries of war, navy, and interior. The new corporation's first task would be to purchase equity in Casoc.[10]

There was ample European precedent for public equity in the oil business, no doubt motivated as much by strategic and political considerations as by financial and commercial ones. Indeed, many of the difficulties encountered by U.S. oil companies in the Middle East were derived from direct political support and equity participation in British and French companies by their own governments. The U.S. experience, however, was just the opposite. Public enterprises such as the Tennessee Valley Authority were the exceptions, not the rule. When Ickes proposed that the United States buy out Casoc's entire equity, the owners opposed the offer on grounds of the traditional noninvolvement of the government in business enterprises. Ickes eventually countered with an offer to buy 70 percent, then 51 percent, and finally 33.33 percent of Casoc. At that stage, negotiations became more serious but ultimately broke down, each side claiming the process was broken off by the other.[11] By then all of the parties had accepted the premise that because oil had become a vital interest to the country's security, some form of government involvement in overseas operations of U.S. oil companies was desirable. The points at issue were the nature and degree of such involvement.

Ickes did not give up so easily. He turned next to an idea originally formulated by a U.S. naval officer visiting the region. To secure Persian Gulf oil supplies, Captain (later Admiral) Andrew Carter had suggested that the U.S. government build a pipeline from the Persian Gulf directly to the Mediterranean. Socal and Texaco (Casoc's owners) supported the idea, even offering to sell the U.S. oil at a discount to transit the pipeline. Ickes also saw the project as a means of strengthening the hand of the United States in negotiating an oil agreement with the British, granting "American oil companies greater protection than they ever had in that area of the world, or where they came in conflict with the British with respect to oil."[12]

Neither of Ickes's schemes for public participation in Saudi Arabian oil materialized. The pipeline idea met strong opposition in Congress and from the U.S. oil companies, and it died a quiet death. To a great degree, oil company opposition came from the smaller, "independent" U.S. firms who felt themselves perpetually squeezed out of upstream (oil-producing) operations by the "major" oil companies, U.S. and foreign alike. Aramco's owners continued to see the commercial advantages of a pipeline, and in July 1945 they organized the Trans-Arabian Pipeline Company (Tapline). Completion of the pipeline was to be delayed another five years, however, while the company negotiated right-of-way and royalty agreements with transit countries (Transjordan, Syria, and Lebanon).

Another delaying factor was the world shortage of steel. The Commerce Department originally had approved an export license for twenty thousand tons of steel, justifying the action on economic, strategic, and political grounds. The Senate Small Business Committee held hearings on the license, however, and concluded that there was no such interest. Not surprisingly, a leading opponent of the export license was the Independent Petroleum Association, representing the smaller, or "independent," oil companies. After these delays, however, steel exports were again authorized shortly before the final Tapline-Syrian agreement was signed in 1949.[13]

The State Department also opposed Ickes's pipeline scheme, believing that it would hinder rather than help in negotiations with Britain over

Middle East oil. Concerned that the United States was shifting from a net exporter of oil to a net importer, the State Department wished to exploit Middle East oil in order to conserve strategically vital U.S. and other Western Hemisphere reserves. Taking this line of reasoning, the State Department's petroleum experts saw an Anglo-American agreement over exploitation of Middle East oil as a cornerstone of U.S. oil diplomacy.

Negotiations toward such an agreement got started in April 1944, but not without considerable suspicion on both sides. The British were convinced that U.S. companies wanted more access to Iraq and Iran, and the Americans feared that the British wished to "horn in" on Saudi Arabia. After hard bargaining, an Anglo-American petroleum agreement was negotiated in August 1944. The agreement was so vague, however, that it appeared likely to offend both Congress and the oil companies.[14] Though submitted to the Senate, it was withdrawn for further "renegotiation" in January 1945. A new draft was completed by September, but it languished in the Senate Foreign Relations Committee until June 1947 and was never submitted to the full Senate for a vote.

The negotiations did have the salutary effect of clearing up many of the suspicions entertained by both the United States and Britain. In the end, however, it was the oil companies themselves that worked out their differences, based more on market than on political conditions.

The U.S. Return to a Supportive Role: 1948–1967

The urgency with which the United States viewed its oil interests in Saudi Arabia was significantly diminished after World War II. This did not mean that U.S. interests in Saudi oil ceased, but rather that—in order of priority—the broader political and strategic threat of communism and Soviet-supported radical nationalism in the region took precedence over oil interests per se in U.S.-Saudi relations.

As a result, efforts to create an active U.S. public-sector role in Saudi oil operations were replaced once again by a policy of indirect government involvement. The United States sought to maintain an overall environment in which the private companies could expand their Saudi and other Middle Eastern operations. The U.S. government also provided direct assistance and support to the companies where it was thought to be in the broader national interest. Two prime examples of the latter are the U.S. role in the purchase of equity shares in Aramco by Jersey Standard (Exxon) and Standard of New York—Socony (Mobil) in 1948 and the government's role in Aramco's 50-50 profit-sharing agreement with Saudi Arabia in 1950.

As Aramco's operations began to expand following the war, its owners, Texaco and Socal, began to consider bringing in other companies in order to supply extra capital for the expansion of operations and also to provide additional markets. It was feared that forcing Saudi oil on Western markets already served by competing companies could lead to price wars and a collapse of the entire oil market. It had been to avoid just such a prospect that the two companies created Caltex in the first place and obtained U.S. government support.

Jersey Standard and Socony were both logical choices to buy into Aramco. Both had worldwide marketing operations and limited Middle East supplies (a jointly shared 23.75 percent equity in IPC). At the same time, both were signatories of the Red Line Agreement, limiting operations in the Middle East. Successful efforts to set aside the Red Line Agreement were conducted for the most part by Jersey Standard and Socony themselves. They had obtained legal opinions at home and in England that the Red Line Agreement had become void during World War II, but they were still worried that their IPC consortium partners might contest their acquisition of Aramco equity by interpreting the two companies' equity in IPC to be based on shares of profits rather than shares of crude. In so doing, the two companies could lose their IPC production, a prospect they wished to avoid.

At this juncture, the U.S. State Department weighed in. During informal Anglo-American oil talks in London in November 1946, the State Department representative asserted that the restrictive clauses in the IPC consortium agreement (that is, the Red Line provisions) were contrary to the Anglo-American Oil Agreement and, moreover, that the U.S. government would support Jersey Standard's and Socony's position that the IPC consortium was based on shares of oil, not shares of profits.[15]

On the domestic side, Jersey Standard, Socony, and Texaco kept in close touch with the Justice Department to insure that the purchase would not contravene U.S. antitrust laws. Attorney General Tom Clark (himself a Texan) told the companies that he saw no objection to the purchase and merely asked to be kept informed.[16]

Intensive and complex bargaining, aided by the support of the U.S. government, removed roadblocks to the purchase one by one, including setting aside the Red Line provisions. Finally, in December 1948, the sale was completed. Socal and Caltex each retained 30 percent of Aramco, Jersey Standard acquired 30 percent, and Socony acquired 10 percent. From the U.S. government point of view, the sale facilitated the continued orderly international oil market process and reinforced U.S. oil security through continued U.S. control of overseas sources.

For the Saudis, Aramco was still a wholly U.S. concession, a major aim of King Abd al-Aziz.[17]

The 50-50 profit-sharing agreement between Aramco and the Saudi Arabian government was somewhat more complicated. By 1950, the Saudis were insisting upon a larger share of Aramco's rapidly growing oil revenues. Their motivation was not simply based on the desire for a higher percentage of profits. The 1933 concession agreement had exempted Aramco (then Casoc) from Saudi taxes and provided for a royalty of four shillings a ton or about $.013 per barrel. By 1948 this had appreciated to $.022 and was then raised to $.033 per barrel, but by the following year, Saudi oil revenues were down by almost 25 percent because of an international dollar shortage and the resulting propensity of sterling countries to buy from British sources.[18]

At the same time, the Saudis were noting better terms obtained by host governments in other oil concessions, including one the Saudis themselves granted in February 1949 to J. Paul Getty's Pacific Western Oil Corporation (later Getty Oil Company) for the Saudi half of the Saudi-Kuwaiti neutral zone. Elsewhere, Venezuela had enacted an income tax on foreign oil companies in 1943 and by 1948 had established a 50-50 profit-sharing principle. The latter appeared increasingly desirable to the Saudis.

In addition to feeling a cash-flow pinch and perceiving that other concessionaires were paying more than Aramco, the Saudis also were sensitive to the amount of taxes Aramco paid to the United States for exploitation of Saudi oil while paying no taxes to the Kingdom. Indeed, in 1949 Aramco paid more to the U.S. Treasury in taxes than it did to Saudi Arabia in royalties.[19]

As a result of all these factors, the Saudi government began in the spring of 1950 to pressure Aramco for more revenues. In August, miffed at what they saw as a lack of response by the company, the Saudis demanded a renegotiation of the concession agreement to provide for an income tax.[20]

In the meantime, the U.S. government was growing concerned over the turn of events. In March 1950, it raised with the British the adverse effect that sterling country restrictions on the purchase of dollar oil were having on Saudi production and revenue. The U.S. ambassador to Saudi Arabia, J. Rives Childs, was also making *démarches* to the Saudis to temper their demands. The State Department realized that some concessions would have to be made but hoped that a spiraling round of royalty hikes, which could destabilize the entire oil market, could be avoided. One tactic the State Department suggested to Aramco was to relinquish parts of their concession that they did not intend to develop in lieu of a royalty hike. Aramco was not at all receptive. The

Getty concession, one of the things that prompted the Saudis to demand higher royalties from Aramco, had itself been relinquished by Aramco.[21]

Aramco was convinced that the Saudis would be satisfied with nothing less than a revenue increase, be it royalties, taxes, or a 50-50 profit sharing such as Venezuela had enacted. Aramco's main concern was double taxation (U.S. and Saudi). The State Department took a dim view of shifting the company's tax burden to the United States by exempting Saudi taxes but said that in any event it was a matter for the Department of Treasury and the Internal Revenue Service to decide.[22]

Matters came to a head in November 1950 when the Saudis announced a 20 percent income tax on all foreign companies. The Aramco owners met with State Department officials to discuss ways to meet the challenge. It was decided that the only course left was to negotiate over terms. In late December, after a month of hard bargaining, Aramco and Saudi Arabia agreed on a 50-50 net profit-sharing arrangement, with royalties and other payments to the Saudis credited against its share. Since the matter of tax exemptions had not yet been settled, Aramco wanted provision also to exempt U.S. taxes from net profits. Later, when the Treasury Department granted an exemption of Saudi profit sharing from Aramco's U.S. tax liability, that provision of the 50-50 agreement was deleted.[23]

The effect of the U.S. Treasury Department's ruling was to transfer Aramco's Saudi tax liability to the United States, precisely what the State Department had earlier hoped to avoid. By 1953, the company's U.S. tax credits completely offset its tax liabilities and it paid no U.S. tax. In later years, this provision was severely criticized as devious and underhanded.[24] There is no question that Aramco's action was completely legal, however. Aramco lawyers took great pains to insure that the 50-50 agreement was drafted to meet the requirements of U.S. tax law.[25] On the economic side, the agreement certainly shifted revenue from the U.S. to the Saudi treasury. The alternatives to the agreement, however, were seen by U.S. government officials as even more harmful to U.S. interests, since they included the possible loss of the oil concession to a U.S. firm entirely. Thus, U.S. government support of the 50-50 agreement was essentially a political decision. The tax exemption was politically justified as necessary to safeguard U.S. access to Saudi Arabia's strategic oil supplies, which, though "owned" by Aramco, ultimately belonged to Saudi Arabia and could not be considered in the same light as U.S. natural resources.

The United States came to Aramco's support once again in the 1950s, and again for strategic reasons. In January 1950, the Saudi Arabian government, in an attempt to increase revenues, concluded an agreement with Greek shipping magnate Aristotle Onassis whereby he could create a private oil tanker company, the Saudi Arabian Tanker Company (Satco). The agreement was amended in April to give Satco a virtual monopoly over the shipment of Saudi oil. Aramco violently opposed the deal as threatening the sanctity of the 1933 concession agreement. The United States joined Britain and other governments in a strong protest to Saudi Arabia for threatening the security and flow of oil shipments vital to the United States and its allies. When the major oil companies retaliated by boycotting Onassis's tanker fleet, the United States gave its tacit support. Ultimately, the Saudis agreed to independent arbitration in 1956, and in 1958 the arbitration found in favor of Aramco.[26]

The Emergence of Saudi Arabia as the Key Supplier: 1967–1974

The period 1967–1974 witnessed more changes in the conduct of international oil transactions than during any previous time since William Knox D'Arcy obtained the first modern oil concession from the shah of Persia in 1901. The intricate set of relationships developed over the years, allowing the major oil companies to dictate oil prices and rates of production, was aimed primarily at preventing a collapse of the international oil market due to an endemic oil glut. Despite the concerns of Ickes and others during World War II that the United States would become a net oil importer, continuing U.S. and foreign discoveries perpetuated the oil glut right through the 1960s.

Market stability throughout the 1960s was maintained by the oil companies' regulating production rates. When a soft market necessitated production reductions, however, the revenues of the producing countries would drop off sharply. As a result, resentment began to grow among the producing countries over their inability to determine or even to regulate their oil revenues.

In 1960, Venezuela, having twice been stung by a lowering of oil prices imposed on it by the oil companies, sought to organize the major oil-exporting countries in order that they could speak with one voice to the companies. Saudi Arabia, also stung by unilateral price reduction by Aramco's owners, was willing to cooperate. As a result of Venezuela's efforts, OPEC was born in September 1960. The time had not yet arrived, however, when OPEC could speak with authority. The main reason was the continuing buyers' market as a result of the oil glut.

The late 1960s saw great changes in supply-demand relationships in the international oil market. The glut had kept prices down, and cheap oil had spurred demand more rapidly than virtually anyone predicted. Western Europe, principally fueled by coal in the nineteenth and early twentieth centuries, had switched to oil. In the United States, the mania for mobility had pushed per capita gasoline consumption to the highest in the world. Even Third World consumption was on the rise. Although new discoveries were still being made, demand was rapidly outstripping supply. By 1970 the United States became a net importer of oil, signaling an end to the oil glut and the beginning of a sellers' market. This set the stage for the oil-producing countries to seize from the companies both ownership of their oil and control over setting prices and production rates.

The process began in 1967. The closure of the Suez Canal and the Trans-Arabian Pipeline during the June 1967 Arab-Israeli war led to a tanker shortage. This put a premium on Libyan crude, valued for its location close to markets in Western Europe as well as for its low sulfur content. King Idris therefore demanded negotiations on the price of Libyan crude. They were begun in September 1969, the month he was overthrown by a group of Libyan army officers that included Colonel Mu'ammar Qadhafi. Negotiations with the new Revolutionary Command Council got under way in 1970.

Because of the tight market, the smaller, independent companies were more vulnerable than the majors, for their oil supplies were less secure. When, after negotiations began, Libya instituted "conservation measures" in May 1970 and cut back production, one of the independents—Occidental—broke ranks. In September 1970 it signed an agreement raising the posted price of Libyan crude and raising the government's tax return from 50 percent to 58 percent. By December, all the operating companies in Libya had capitulated to Libyan demands.[27]

The implications of the Libyan victory were not immediately apparent to the major oil-consuming countries. They had for years been content to leave price and production-rate negotiations to the oil companies and "were ill-equipped to understand that Libya's success would seriously undermine the negotiating strength of the companies."[28]

This lack of understanding was illustrated in the debate that arose in the United States at the time over what had happened and what was in store. To Ambassador James E. Akins, the Libyan success ushered in a brand-new era in the world oil market, "like a flash of lightning in a summer sky."[29] Professor M. A. Adelman, on the other hand, questioned the existence of an oil shortage and suggested that the oil companies themselves had more to gain than lose in creating a shortage to drive up prices, despite an abundance of proved reserves.[30] Moreover, Adelman was critical of the State Department for not intervening in the Libyan case, claiming that the United States could easily have induced the oil companies to prepare a common course of action for defeating Libya's demands. Adelman claimed that at the time of the negotiations, the oil-producing countries were not prepared for an open confrontation.[31]

With the benefit of hindsight, one might conclude that the immediate events surrounding the Libyan negotiations could have been altered by prompt U.S. action, although Adelman wholly underestimates the difficulties involved even if such a decision had been made. Nevertheless, the underlying shift in the terms of trade from a buyers' to a sellers' market probably means that defeating Libya's demands would merely have postponed the shift in the control of prices and production rates from the companies to the producing countries. Given the rapidly expanding demand for oil at pre-1973 price levels, moreover, that day would probably have come sooner rather than later.

The Libyan success quickly led to demands for higher prices and higher tax rates from all the oil-producing states. At the OPEC meeting in Caracas in December 1970, a warning was issued to the companies that unless OPEC's demands were met, its members would take concerted action. In the face of this threat, the oil companies met in New York in January 1971 to come up with a concerted strategy on their part. Meeting with them were representatives of the Department of State, which approved of joint company action, and the Department of Justice, which assured the companies that they would not be prosecuted for violation of U.S. antitrust laws.[32] The companies then created the London Policy Group, again with U.S. backing, to coordinate the negotiations on a worldwide basis. In the Middle East, OPEC divided itself into a Persian Gulf and a Mediterranean group, each negotiating separately. The willingness of the companies to deal collectively with OPEC members was itself a departure from the 1960s when the companies, from a position of strength, insisted on dealing with the producing countries on an individual, bilateral basis.

It is possible that even at this juncture the United States could have successfully countered OPEC's challenge to the companies, had it actively sought a confrontation. However, the United States had multiple interests to pursue, among the Gulf producers in particular. More of these interests involved cooperation than confrontation. Thus, when Under Secretary of State John Irwin visited Iran, Saudi Arabia, and Kuwait in mid-January 1971, seeking assurances of continued supplies at reasonable prices, no strong pressures were brought to bear.[33]

Ambassador Douglas MacArthur II in Tehran, anxious not to offend the shah, expressed concern that in negotiating collectively the companies were seeking to "play OPEC members against one another," which was indeed the basis of their strategy. On MacArthur's recommendation, Secretary of State William Rogers communicated U.S. support for separate negotiations.[34] With U.S. and also British support for the companies' united front withdrawn, the London Policy Group position collapsed, and on February 14, 1971, the companies signed an agreement in Tehran generally capitulating to the demands of the Gulf-state producers. The same month, Algeria took control of 51 percent of French producing interests (accounting for about 70 percent of production), with compensation minus unilaterally imposed taxes. In March, Libya signed individual agreements with its producing companies on terms compatible with the Tehran agreement. It was all over. OPEC had seized total control of oil pricing from the companies. Although bilateral company–oil-producing country negotiations continued for some time afterward, unilateral decisions by the producing countries became the determinant of price and production setting.

At the same time that the oil-producing countries were gaining control over price setting, they were also gaining control over ownership of the oil granted through concessions to the oil companies. Some states—such as Algeria, Iraq, and Libya—accomplished this through nationalization. Saudi Arabia and the Gulf states preferred to follow the route of "participation," a term coined by Saudi Minister of Petroleum and Mineral Resources Ahmad Zaki Yamani, in 1967.[35] Proponents of participation envisaged an increased proportion of oil revenues to the oil-producing states, assertion of national sovereignty over all aspects of production, continued use of the oil companies to restrict supply and raise revenues, and investment in distribution and marketing (downstream) operations.[36]

Yamani explained that participation was infinitely better than nationalization because it kept the companies in the game, so to speak, and maintained an incentive for them to continue to restrict production rates in order to maintain price stability. Otherwise, once the companies lost their equity in upstream operations, they would lose interest in maintaining stable prices, and all would suffer.

A commitment to the principle of participation was accepted at the OPEC meeting in Vienna in June 1968. At the July 1971 OPEC meeting, also in Vienna, a resolution was passed calling for immediate steps to implement the principle of participation. Soon thereafter, participation negotiations began. The producing states were led by Yamani, and the companies were represented by the Aramco partners (Socal, Texaco, Mobil, and Exxon). After extensive and hard bargaining, a General Agreement on Participation was completed in December 1972 and accepted by Saudi Arabia, Qatar, and the United Arab Emirates (UAE) in early 1973. The agreement was extremely complex: Basically it called for the host countries to acquire 25 percent equity in the companies' upstream operations, gradually increasing the share to 100 percent. Crude oil from the operations was divided into "participation crude"—that part owned by the countries that could be sold on the open market; "buy-back crude"—the part the countries owned but were to sell back to the companies to market (buy-back crude was further subdivided by pricing arrangements); and "equity crude"—the part that companies still owned.[37]

The participation agreements were generally viewed as transitional in nature, preparing the way for eventual producing-country ownership. The Saudis increased their share to 60 percent ownership of Aramco in 1974 and in 1980 finally assumed full ownership. Aramco nevertheless functions much as before under Saudi control, and the interests of its four owners remain an incentive to oil company–producing country cooperation. The final takeover, however, was not so significant as the original participation agreement, for it was the latter that secured Saudi control over its national oil resources.

In the fall and winter of 1973-1974, three events took place that were to focus international attention on Saudi Arabian oil policies. In September 1973, OPEC called for negotiations with the companies to raise the price of oil. When they were convened in Vienna on October 8, OPEC members demanded a 100 percent price increase. The companies were powerless to resist and broke off negotiations on October 12. On October 16, the Gulf producers met in Kuwait and unilaterally raised posted prices 70 percent.

In the meantime, on October 6, the October 1973 Arab-Israeli war broke out. For almost a year previously, Saudis from King Faysal on down had been warning that unless some progress was made on a Middle East peace settlement that recognized Arab rights, the Arabs would be obliged to use oil as a political instrument—the oil weapon. Thus, when the war broke out, the United States made a special effort to assure King Faysal of its intention to remain evenhanded. On October 19, however, President Richard Nixon asked Congress for $2.2 billion in military aid to Israel. To Faysal, this appeared to be a betrayal of U.S. assurances, and the following day, under the aegis of the Organization of Arab Petroleum Exporting Countries (OAPEC), he instituted the Arab oil embargo.

The embargo was an economic response to a basically political problem. It did have some important consequences, however, for U.S.-Saudi oil relations. The most important one was a second price rise. Taking advantage of the tight supply situation created by the embargo, OPEC price hawks, led by Iran, raised the price of oil an additional 130 percent at the December OPEC meeting. Marker crude that cost $3.01 per barrel on October 1 and $5.12 per barrel on October 16 was increased to $11.65 per barrel as of January 1, 1974.[38]

Ironically, the Saudis, who through the embargo had made the second price hike possible, were not themselves price hawks. Although they were firmly convinced that oil, as a wasting asset, had been greatly underpriced by the companies, they feared that too abrupt a rise in prices could create major dislocations in the free world economy, with serious political implications as well. That they were the instrument for the success of the price hawks in doubling the price of oil a second time in three months is another example of how the pursuit of multiple interests (in this case oil interests and regional Arab political interests) created an ambivalent outcome from the Saudi point of view.

The embargo forced the United States for the first time to focus on the necessity for developing an integrated energy policy, taking into account domestic as well as foreign supply-and-demand factors. The realization that the United States was dependent on foreign oil to maintain its energy-intensive standard of living and that the era of cheap energy was over came slowly and painfully to Americans who had come to believe that personal mobility was their right.

Domestically, the U.S. government focused in the near term on allocation, attempting to restrict private consumption more severely than industrial consumption.[39] It did so through a series of measures that included the creation of the Federal Energy Office, later replaced by the Federal Energy Administration (FEA), which in turn was later absorbed into the Department of Energy. The "success" of the restrictive policy was reflected in the long lines at the gas pumps.

Domestic policy over the longer term had evolved by November 1974 into a program of conservation and development of alternative forms of energy. Spearheading that policy was Project Independence, a major government study undertaken by FEA. Begun in March and involving over five hundred professionals, it was an attempt to evaluate various energy strategies that could enable the United States to become independent of foreign sources by 1985.[40] Although, in retrospect, the project's name and ultimate goal were unrealizable, the framework and analytical tools developed in the process were a valuable contribution to a newly pressing national interest, insuring a reliable supply of energy and reasonable prices.

The formulation of foreign policy responses to the embargo evolved more slowly. Secretary of State Henry Kissinger tried and failed in November 1973 to persuade a vacillating King Faysal to rescind the embargo. In December 1973, Kissinger made his widely publicized remarks about the possibility of a military response in case of the "strangulation" of the industrial world.[41] The statement brought instant and bitter reaction from the Arab world but no results.

By the time the Saudis called off the embargo on March 18, 1974, the United States had finally begun to focus on the fundamental issues of oil price and production setting. It also had come to realize that it must develop government-to-government energy relations and that the days in which it could depend on the international oil companies for this function were over. The companies were no longer influential. Moreover, Saudi Arabia—with its high productive capacity and extensive proved reserves, its small population and low absorptive capacity for capital—emerged as the key country in OPEC's ability to set prices.

U.S. foreign energy policy was both multilateral, focusing on the major oil consumers, and bilateral, focusing on the major oil exporter, Saudi Arabia. The principal assumption appeared to be that if consumption could be curbed and Saudi Arabia could be persuaded to maintain production levels so as not to reinstitute an "artificial" shortage, the energy gap would disappear. With a surplus of oil, OPEC price discipline would be broken.[42] In February 1974, the United States hosted the Washington Energy Conference, attended by the European Economic Community members, Canada, Japan, and Norway. Because of the concern of some participants that they might alienate the oil producers, either by appearing to participate in an oil consumers' cartel or by associating with U.S. policies in support of Israel while the embargo was still in progress, the conference was only a moderate success. It did establish an Energy Coordinating Group that ultimately came up with an international energy program. In November 1974, the program was completed. It established an International Energy Agency (IEA) and, more important, established an oil-sharing agreement in case of another emergency.[43] U.S. efforts to dissuade other major consumers from making bilateral arrangements with the producing countries failed, however. France, Britain, West Germany, and Italy all negotiated separate agreements early in the embargo.[44]

Efforts to influence Saudi oil policy achieved mixed results. Although U.S.-Saudi political relations did indeed result in Saudi moderation, the often intense U.S. efforts to persuade the Saudis to moderate prices in OPEC coincided in large measure with the Saudis' own interests in doing so. Not only were the Saudis concerned that overpricing oil would have serious international economic consequences, but they were determined to play the key price and production role in OPEC. Petroleum Minister Yamani frequently discussed with Americans in public and private positions the Saudi compulsion to be "the leader" in price and production affairs. He would point out that this was the natural result of their large reserves position and that it was far more in the U.S. interest to have Saudi Arabia in the lead rather than an irresponsible country like Libya. The Saudi leadership required the Saudis to produce beyond their revenue needs in a tight market, to moderate the upward pressure on prices, and to cut production in a soft market to keep prices from collapsing. Their high productive capacity and relatively moderate capital requirements allowed them to do this.

The Years of OPEC Ascendancy: 1974–1979

Between 1974 and 1978, largely due to Saudi leadership, the price of oil actually fell in absolute terms (that is, the rise in oil prices was less than the rate of inflation). At the December 1976 OPEC meeting in Doha, both Saudi Arabia and Abu Dhabi broke ranks and increased the price of their crude only 5 percent, compared to 10 percent for the others.[45] In order to keep the price stable, they raised production to nine million b/d in 1977. By mid-year, a compromise was worked out among the OPEC members whereby Saudi Arabia and Abu Dhabi raised prices 5 percent in return for a price freeze that lasted until December 1978, almost one and one-half years.

By late 1978, however, the internal situation in Iran had deteriorated drastically, and it seemed only a matter of time before the shah would be ousted. Iranian oil production, which had been at 5.8 million b/d in July 1982, dropped to 2.3 million b/d in December and would plunge to 440 thousand b/d in January 1979. In response to this crisis, spot oil market prices began to climb. At the December 1978 OPEC meeting in Abu Dhabi, Saudi Arabia was instrumental in obtaining agreement for gradually increasing posted prices from $12.91 to $14.55 per barrel.[46] The agreement failed to hold up. With the two-month hiatus in Iranian production (January and February 1979), panic buying spread throughout the market. Moreover, companies and countries alike, remembering the 1973-1974 period, began to build up inventories beyond normal levels in order not to be caught in another supply squeeze. This factor was particularly disastrous, for stocks had been allowed to run down during 1978 (a stable market period) in order to save money on high storage costs and to avoid high interest rates.

In the meantime, the Saudis, who had raised production from around 7.5 million b/d in the summer of 1978 to 10.4 million b/d in December as Iranian production declined, announced in January 1979 that they would limit production to 9.5 million b/d and in April announced an 8.5 million b/d ceiling. These announcements served to place even more upward pressure on prices, and by the end of 1979, the price had risen to $23.55.

Various explanations have been given for the Saudis' behavior, from simple greed to Saudi irritation with the United States, particularly over U.S. pressure to associate the Saudis with the Camp David agreement.[47] Another explanation put forward focused on Saudi fears that sustained production at near peak capacity could cause irreparable losses to their recoverable reserves. The technical aspects of Saudi production were subject to a great deal of sensitivity at the time, in light of the Saudi government's taking control of production management from Aramco.[48]

None of these explanations alone can adequately explain Saudi policies that were in apparent contradiction to its intention to maintain prices. Charges of Saudi greed ignore the fact that in 1976-1977, Saudi Arabia had priced its crude well under what other countries were charging. Political motivation may have had more to do with lowering the ceiling, although even then the ceiling was not strictly followed. Production remained at 9.8 million b/d in the first quarter of 1979, then dropped to 8.8 million b/d for April through May before going back up to 9.8 million b/d for the rest of the year.[49] Moreover, by April, Iranian production had recovered to 3.6 million b/d, exceeding November levels. By July both OPEC and world production had fully recovered, yet the price continued to rise.[50]

Conservation also probably played a role. Not only were the Saudis concerned about the technical aspects of production, but in February 1978 they had already set what amounted to an 8.5 million b/d ceiling by requiring that their light crude compose no more than 65 percent of total production. This move was intended to bring light-crude production in line with the estimated proportion of light to heavy crude, both to conserve more valuable light crude and to place less strain on Saudi Arabia's primary field, the Ghawar field.[51]

The Saudis were also concerned that with high world inflation the oil was worth more in the ground than out. Saudi Minister of Planning Hisham Nazer said in 1978 that the country could meet its reserve needs by exporting only five million b/d.[52] With revenues exceeding expenditures and foreign-exchange balances mounting, many Saudi conservationists argued that Saudi oil production was much too high.[53] These pressures were certainly felt by the Saudi leadership, but had to be balanced against the other economic, political, and technical concerns that made up the decision to reimpose a ceiling in 1979. It is doubtful, given the compartmental and informal nature of Saudi decision making, whether these factors were ever rationalized in a formal manner prior to the decision. In retrospect, the decision did exacerbate the price rises of 1979, but it neither created the market conditions nor was even the primary factor in the price rises. A more debilitating influence on the market was the atmosphere of panic surrounding the Iranian crisis and the determination of the OPEC price hawks to take advantage of it.

During the years following the Arab embargo, the United States also attempted, but without success, to persuade Saudi Arabia to raise its productive capacity in order to provide for anticipated increases in demands. The Americans were apparently concerned that unless expansion plans were begun early, they could not be completed soon enough to avoid another energy crunch. Various studies during the late 1970s speculated that Saudi capacity would have to reach twenty million b/d by 1990 to keep up with world demand. Saudi Petroleum Minister Zaki Yamani rejected that figure out of hand.[54] The Saudis believed that were they to increase their capacity to such an extent, pressure on them to produce at near capacity would be almost intolerable in a future oil crisis. Such a move would not only obviate the need for the major consumers to discipline their own energy requirements but would also accelerate the depletion of Saudi Arabia's only major natural resource.

The Oil Glut of the 1980s

The price escalation of 1979 fulfilled Saudi warnings that overpricing would inevitably result in a decline in demand. World production peaked in December 1979. Even so the price continued to rise from $23.55 in the fourth quarter of 1979 to over $34.00 in 1981. The Saudis continued to produce at 9.8 million b/d to keep prices from rising even higher. Then in September 1980, the Iran-Iraq war broke out, with a subsequent shutting in of Iranian and Iraqi production. Immediately fears arose that a new energy crisis was on the way. To forestall it, Saudi Arabia increased production to 10.3 million b/d in November, holding at around that figure until the following August. The high rate of production was maintained basically to force the price hawks to lower prices. Although some price hawks were charging $36.00, the Saudis maintained their price at $32.00 per barrel.

By August 1981, however, it had become obvious that, unlike the Iranian crisis, the Iran-Iraq war had occurred on the downside of a market cycle and had merely postponed the coming oil glut by about a year. Beginning in September 1981, the Saudis began to cut production. In the December 1981 OPEC meeting, a new $34 price was agreed upon, but as demand continued to decline in 1982, even that became difficult to support. Moreover, as revenues declined, many oil producers began to offer "discounts" for their oil. Iran in particular expressed willingness to sell to anyone at greatly reduced prices. To maintain even a semblance of price unity, the Saudis continued to cut production, reaching around 4.5 million b/d by the beginning of 1983. OPEC was again in disarray. Its difficulties were increased when companies and countries that had added to the price escalation by stocking in 1979 now added to the softening in demand by destocking in 1982.

As the OPEC price cut in March 1983 and continued price and production discipline in 1984 indicate, OPEC was not in as dire danger of collapse as some of its critics predicted. Nevertheless, as an instrument for maintaining market stability, its effectiveness has never matched either the efforts of the major oil companies worldwide or those of the Texas Railroad Commission, which performed the same function in the United States in an earlier era.

In just a decade since the producing countries had seized control of their oil resources, and OPEC, with Saudi Arabia at the helm, had seized control of price and production setting, the world had witnessed two rapid price escalations and two oil gluts. Despite everyone's vociferous support for market stability, it appeared to be as far from realization in 1984 as in 1973, and no one could rule out yet another energy crisis at the end of the latest glut. For the United States, the world's greatest consuming country, and Saudi Arabia, the world's greatest exporting country, oil relations would remain a vital mutual interest for some time to come.

Notes

1. Aaron David Miller, *Search for Security: Saudi Arabian Oil and American Foreign Policy, 1939–1949* (Chapel Hill: University of North Carolina Press, 1980), p. 7. See also John DeNovo, "The Movement for Aggressive American Oil Policy Abroad, 1918–1920," *American Historical Review* 61 (July 1956), pp. 854–876.

2. For a discussion of these events, see Miller, *Search for Security,* pp. 3–16; and George W. Stocking, *Middle East Oil: A Study in Political and Economic Controversy* (Nashville, Tenn.: Vanderbilt University Press, 1970), pp. 40–65.

3. U.S. Department of State, *Foreign Relations of the United States,* vol. 2 (Washington, D.C.: Government Printing Office, 1922), p. 338 (hereafter cited as *FRUS,* with volume and date).

4. Stocking, *Middle East Oil,* p. 55.

5. Ibid.

6. Miller, *Search for Security,* p. 12.

7. See H. St. John B. Philby, *Arabian Oil Ventures* (Washington, D.C.: Middle East Institute, 1964), pp. 67–68.

8. For an account of Saudi public finance during this period, see David E. Long, *The Hajj Today: A Survey of the Contemporary Makkah Pilgrimage* (Albany: State University of New York Press, 1979).

9. Miller, *Search for Security,* p. 21. For a discussion of the terms of the 1933 concession agreement, see Donald Wells, "ARAMCO: The Evolution of an Oil Concession," in Raymond F. Mikesell, ed., *Foreign Investment in the*

Petroleum and Mineral Industries (Baltimore and London: Johns Hopkins University Press, 1971), pp. 216–219.

10. U.S. Congress, Senate, *Petroleum Arrangements with Saudi Arabia,* hearings before a Special Committee Investigating the National Defense Program, pt. 41, 80th Cong., 1st sess., 1948 (Washington, D.C.: Government Printing Office, 1948), pp. 25237–25238.

11. Ibid., p. 24234. See also Stocking, *Middle East Oil,* pp. 98–99; and Miller, *Search for Security,* pp. 74–81 and 250, n. 75.

12. U.S. Congress, Senate, *Petroleum Arrangements,* p. 25247.

13. Stocking, *Middle East Oil,* pp. 102–103.

14. Miller, *Search for Security,* p. 258, n. 56.

15. *FRUS,* vol. 8, 1946, pp. 38–46.

16. U.S. Congress, Senate, Select Committee on Small Business, *The International Petroleum Cartel* (Washington, D.C.: Government Printing Office, 1952), p. 121n. See David Sidney Painter, "The Politics of Oil: Multinational Oil Corporations and United States Foreign Policy, 1941–1954" (Ph.D. dissertation, University of North Carolina at Chapel Hill, 1982), pp. 239–264; Burton I. Kaufman, *The Oil Cartel Case: A Documentary Study of Antitrust Activity in the Cold War Era* (Westport, Conn.: Greenwood Press, 1978), pp. 27–28.

17. *FRUS,* vol. 5, 1948, pp. 64–66.

18. Painter, "The Politics of Oil," p. 448.

19. *FRUS,* vol. 5, 1950, pp. 52, 56–57.

20. Ibid., pp. 59–76.

21. Ibid., pp. 76–96.

22. Ibid., pp. 106–109.

23. Wells, *ARAMCO,* p. 220.

24. See U.S. Congress, Senate, *Multinational Corporations and United States Foreign Policy; Hearings Before the Subcommittee on Multinational Corporations of the Committee on Foreign Relations,* pts. 7 and 8, 93rd Cong., 2d sess., 1975 (Washington, D.C.: Government Printing Office, 1975).

25. Ibid., pt. 8, pp. 350–358.

26. For an account of the affair, see Malcolm Peck, "Saudi Arabia in United States Foreign Policy to 1958: A Case Study in the Sources and Determinants of American Policy" (Ph.D. dissertation, Fletcher School of Law and Diplomacy, 1970), p. 245; David Holden and Richard Johns, *The House of Saud* (London: Sidgwick and Jackson, 1981), pp. 180–182; and C. L. Sulzberger, "U.S. Studies Onassis Monopoly for Shipping Saudi Arabia's Oil," *New York Times,* June 23, 1954.

27. Richard Chadbourn Weisberg, *The Politics of Crude Oil Pricing in the Middle East, 1970–1975: A Study in International Bargaining,* Research Series no. 31 (Berkeley: Institute of International Studies, University of California, 1977), pp. 38–48.

28. Ibid., p. 50.

29. James E. Akins, "The Oil Crisis: This Time the Wolf Is Here," *Foreign Affairs* 51, no. 3 (April 1973), p. 471.

30. M. A. Adelman, "Is the Oil Shortage Real? Oil Companies as OPEC Tax Collectors," *Foreign Policy* 9 (Winter 1972-1973), pp. 69–107.

31. Ibid., pp. 79–80.
32. U.S. Congress, Senate, *Multinational Corporations,* pt. 9, pp. 46–49.
33. Weisberg, *The Politics of Crude Oil Pricing,* p. 57.
34. Ibid., p. 59, citing U.S. Congress, Senate, *Multinational Corporations,* pt. 6, p. 66, exhibit 4.
35. I first heard Yamani's discussion of the subject with the U.S. ambassador, Hermann Fr. Eilts, at Yamani's winter home at Hada, near Taif, Saudi Arabia, in 1967. It was also the subject of a lecture by Yamani at the American University of Beirut.
36. Weisberg, *The Politics of Crude Oil Pricing,* p. 78.
37. Ibid., p. 81.
38. The January 1974 price rise was actually agreed upon by OPEC on December 22, 1973. See U.S. Department of State, Office of the Historian, "The Evolution of OPEC, 1959–1983," Historical Research Project no. 1349. pp. 10–11.
39. See U.S. Federal Energy Administration (FEA), Office of Economic Impact, "The Economic Impact of the Oil Embargo on the American Economy" (Washington, D.C.: FEA, August 8, 1974).
40. See U.S. Federal Energy Administration, "Project Independence: A Summary" (Washington, D.C.: Government Printing Office, November 1974).
41. *Business Week,* January 13, 1975, p. 67.
42. Weisberg, *The Politics of Crude Oil Pricing,* p. 129.
43. Ibid., pp. 127–128.
44. Ibid., p. 126.
45. Holden and Johns, *The House of Saud,* pp. 450–451.
46. Extracted from figures in the *Petroleum Economist,* 1979.
47. For a brief summary of these various arguments and their protagonists, see William B. Quandt, *Saudi Arabia's Oil Policy: A Staff Paper* (Washington, D.C.: Brookings Institution, 1982), pp. 15–21.
48. See David E. Long, "Saudi Oil Policy," *Wilson Quarterly* 3 (Winter 1979), pp. 88–89.
49. Quandt, *Saudi Arabia's Oil Policy,* p. 14, table 1.
50. Extrapolated from *Petroleum Economist,* 1979.
51. Long, "Saudi Oil Policy," pp. 90–91.
52. Ibid., p. 86.
53. This premise was also challenged by Saudi Arabia's critics. See Quandt, *Saudi Arabia's Oil Policy,* p. 7.
54. Long, "Saudi Oil Policy," p. 91.

3
U.S.-Saudi Military Relations

For many Americans the U.S. congressional debate over the sale of F-15 fighter aircraft to Saudi Arabia in 1981 was the first occasion on which they realized that there were U.S.-Saudi military relations. In fact, relations in the areas of military assistance and cooperation predated the F-15 sale by almost forty years. Originating in the midst of World War II, the military relationship waned at the war's end but gained a renewed importance with the mutual U.S. and Saudi perceptions of the Soviet threat to the region that began in the late 1940s. Their perceptions have persisted to the present day.

The Early Years: 1943–1953

Military relations were formally initiated on February 18, 1943, when the United States declared Saudi Arabia eligible for U.S. Lend-Lease aid.[1] The action was taken in order to extend desperately needed hard currency to the Kingdom and was justified on strategic grounds. According to a letter from Secretary of State Cordell Hull to the Lend-Lease administrator:

> Saudi Arabia lies between the vital Red Sea and Persian Gulf shipping routes and across the direct air route to India and the Far East. The Government of Saudi Arabia has been highly sympathetic to the cause of the United Nations and has accorded United States Army aircraft the right to fly over certain uninhabited zones of Saudi Arabia. Furthermore, the Army may at any time wish to obtain extensive air facilities in Saudi Arabia. However, the State Department is of the opinion that it will be difficult to obtain additional privileges from the Government of Saudi Arabia unless we are prepared to furnish certain direct assistance to that country.[2]

As a part of the Lend-Lease program, a U.S. military survey team led by General Ralph Royce was sent to the Kingdom to determine Saudi military needs. It was followed by a small advisory mission headed by Colonel Garret B. Shomber, who arrived in April 1944. The Americans were supposed to be part of a joint U.S.–United Kingdom mission, but Anglo-American rivalries caused each country to send a separate mission.

The "extensive air facilities" mentioned by Hull began to materialize after a good deal of hard bargaining and competition with the British. On August 5 and 6, 1945, the United States and Saudi Arabia reached an agreement for the construction of an air base at Dhahran (and emergency airfields at Lauqa and Hafr al-Batin). The agreement was concluded in Riyadh by an exchange of notes between the Saudi acting foreign minister, Yusuf Yassin, and the U.S. minister, Colonel William A. Eddy. The United States agreed to turn over the Dhahran air base to Saudi Arabia at the end of the three-year period following the end of hostilities against Japan.[3]

Following the war, the Dhahran airfield greatly declined in importance. By 1949, however, with the advent of the cold war and the Soviet threat to the area, it regained its strategic importance. Moreover, Saudi Arabia's oil production—still small but growing—served to enhance the Kingdom's overall strategic importance. Oil-field security was a major element of Saudi economic interests, and protection from foreign threats, particularly Soviet-orchestrated regional instability, dominated Saudi military security interests. These two interests—oil security and the Soviet threat—became and have remained the cornerstone of U.S. military relations with Saudi Arabia.

On June 23, 1949, again after long, hard bargaining, the United States and Saudi Arabia concluded a second agreement that stipulated the terms of U.S. access to the Dhahran airfield.[4] The airfield had been formally turned over to the Saudis the previous March. At the time of the agreement, a U.S. military survey team was established at Saudi request to make recommendations to the Kingdom for the formation of a Saudi armed force. Great Britain had established a military training mission two years earlier to create a lightly mechanized force of some ten thousand men, but as the Saudis looked more toward the United States, the British mission was phased out in 1951.

Major General Richard O'Keefe, USAF, headed the military survey team that traveled forty-four thousand miles in the Kingdom between September 1 and October 22, 1949, collecting basic strategic data. The team recommended training and equipping, over a five-year period, a Saudi Arabian defense force of some 43,000 officers and men, composed of 28,000 combat troops and 15,000 air force personnel. It did not, however, recommend offensive mechanized equipment such as tanks or fighter aircraft. Some modest naval installations were also considered.

The O'Keefe report thus became the first comprehensive U.S. plan for building a modern Saudi armed force.

The Saudis approved the 1949 Dhahran airfield agreement and the recommendations of the O'Keefe mission survey despite deep bitterness over the U.S. role in the creation of Israel in 1948. Saudi resentment over U.S. support of Israel was outweighed by the continuing perception of encircling external threats to Saudi security and by the desire for a U.S. commitment for protection against such threats. At that time, the Saudis believed that the principal threat came from the Hashimite kingdoms of Jordan and Iraq.[5]

Over the years external threats to the Kingdom have changed, but the Saudi desire for U.S. military support against encirclement has persisted. Resentment at what Saudis believed to be overweening U.S. support of Israel has also persisted, however, and has created an ambivalence that has permeated U.S.-Saudi military relations from that day to this.

The 1949 Dhahran Air Field Agreement was to be in force for one year when it was to be replaced with a more detailed agreement following submission of the O'Keefe report and recommendations for U.S. military assistance to the Kingdom. Because negotiations for the new agreement did not begin until December 1950 and quickly bogged down, the 1949 agreement was extended an additional year. The major points of contention included levels of assistance, the amount of U.S. grant aid in contrast to reimbursable assistance, questions of extraterritoriality and Saudi sovereignty, and the duration of the access agreement (the United States wanted a twenty-five-year lease).

The two countries finally concluded the new agreement on June 18, 1951, through an exchange of notes by the U.S. ambassador and the Saudi foreign minister. It provided for U.S. use of the Dhahran airfield for five years and was extendable for five more years.[6] A Mutual Defense Assistance Agreement was signed at the same time, laying the groundwork for a U.S. military training mission and arms deliveries.[7]

The creation of the U.S. Military Training Mission (USMTM) was the principal military assistance component of the Mutual Defense Assistance Agreement. A U.S. Mutual Defense Assistance Program survey team arrived in the Kingdom on July 17, 1951, to prepare recommendations on the size and the nature of the training mission. Its recommendations ultimately led to the formal establishment of USMTM–Saudi Arabia on June 27, 1953, by means of an exchange of notes between the U.S. ambassador and the Saudi minister of defense and aviation that implemented the Mutual Defense Assistance Agreement of 1951.[8] The military training mission became and remains the principal instrument of U.S. military relations with Saudi Arabia.

In the broadest sense, the U.S.-Saudi military relations during the decade from 1943 to 1953 involved a trade-off between the U.S. desire for access to a forward strategic military base and the Saudi desire for evidence and reassurance of a U.S. commitment to protect the regime against foreign threats. There was ambivalence on both sides. The United States did not want its military commitment to Saudi Arabia to become so broadly construed that it could be seen as a carte blanche and possibly entangle the United States in regional conflicts beyond the scope of the relationship. Particularly, the United States did not want its military relations with Saudi Arabia to place it in a position where it had to choose sides on the Arab-Israeli issue.

Saudi ambivalence toward the United States, on the other hand, stemmed not only from what the Kingdom perceived to be unevenhanded U.S. support of Israel and from anxiety over the strength of the U.S. commitment to protect the Saudi regime, but also from considerations of Saudi and broader Arab national pride. The Saudis were, and remain, highly sensitive to any perceived infringement of their sovereignty as well as to charges of other Arab states that they had relinquished any portion of sovereignty to a foreign power by granting base rights.

The Saud Years: 1953–1962

On November 9, 1953, less than five months after the formal establishment of the U.S. Military Training Mission to Saudi Arabia, King Abd al-Aziz, creator of the modern Kingdom, died. His son, Saud bin Abd al-Aziz, was immediately proclaimed king. The reign of King Saud proved to be stormy for Saudi Arabia and for U.S.-Saudi military relations as well. King Saud's reign came at a time when Saudi Arabia's rapidly expanding oil wealth made the Kingdom increasingly more difficult to administer. At the same time, the winds of radical Arab nationalism, fanned by the charismatic leadership of Egypt's President Nasser, began blowing across the entire Middle East. The king endeavored to cement good relations with Nasser, visiting Cairo in the spring of 1954 and agreeing on June 11 of that year to a "unified command" with Egypt.[9]

In January 1955, an Egyptian military training mission arrived in the Kingdom, which temporarily overshadowed USMTM in its influence on the Saudi military. Unfortunately for the Saudis, the Egyptians introduced excessively rigid administrative techniques characterized by "red tape" and applied training methods based on rote memorization that were not only at variance with the Americans' more heuristic approach, but inhibited troop-level initiative and creativity so necessary to a modern fighting force.[10]

Saudi-Egyptian relations in the 1950s, until they began to sour in 1958, were a major impediment not only to U.S.-Saudi military relations, but to U.S.-Saudi relations in general. King Saud was also highly suspicious of British intentions in Jordan, Iraq, and the Gulf. He still believed that Jordan and Iraq, former British protectorates and under strong British influence, constituted major threats to Saudi Arabia. The Kingdom also continued to press its claim to Buraymi Oasis (see discussion in Chapter 5). These factors all played at least some part in keeping Saudi Arabia out of the U.S.- and British-sponsored Baghdad Pact in 1955.[11]

Despite heightened U.S.-Saudi tensions and King Saud's attempts to play the Egyptians and Americans off against each other, the Saudis still sought U.S. arms. They wished to maintain a military relationship, in large part as earnest of a U.S. commitment to protect the regime.

For the United States, extending the 1951 Dhahran Air Field Agreement was a major military aim in the relationship. However, although the strategic value of the airfield was still an important U.S. interest, it was not an overriding one. The Dhahran facility had cost about $50 million to build and probably could not have been duplicated, even in the late 1950s, for twice that amount. Even though the United States wanted to retain access to the Dhahran airfield, it was not willing to pay any price to do so.

The 1951 Dhahran agreement expired before a new agreement could be reached. The United States was allowed to stay, however, on a month-to-month basis while the negotiations dragged on. One area of hard bargaining was over arms transfers. The O'Keefe report did not include recommendations for any mechanized offensive equipment, but the Saudis construed informal technical discussions as a sign of U.S. willingness to develop, inter alia, a modest force of fighter aircraft. This was probably the first of many instances in which technical discussions were considered as informal, albeit real, U.S. commitments.

During the period prior to the expiration of the 1951 agreement, the United States did agree to major arms transfers of M-41 light tanks and a number of B-26 bombers, both items that were obsolete. The Saudis received six B-26s following the signing of the 1953 agreement. In early 1955, as the time for renewing the Dhahran Air Field Agreement began to approach, the United States agreed to the sale of three additional B-26s. The Saudis acquired aircraft mainly for show, and because the nascent Saudi air force could not absorb them, they fell quickly into disrepair, an embarrassing situation for both countries.

The sale of tanks was briefly enmeshed in a more ticklish problem. Increased Arab-Israeli tension had obliged Saudi Arabia to join an Arab "defensive alliance" in October 1955, resulting in increased Jewish

American protests to the proposed tank sale. The press, the Congress, and the Israeli ambassador to the United States, Abba Eban, all criticized the sale. Criticism reached a peak on February 16, 1956, the day before the tanks were to be shipped. Realizing the potential damage to U.S.-Saudi relations if the transaction failed to go through, the Eisenhower administration sought to muster congressional support while temporarily suspending shipment. On February 18, 1956, Under Secretary of State Herbert Hoover, Jr., lobbied key senators, including Senator William Knowland of California and Senator Walter George of Georgia, chairman of the Senate Foreign Relations Committee. Though agreeing that the tanks should be sent, they were unenthusiastic about taking criticism from the "pro-Israel lobby."[12] Nevertheless, the suspension was lifted, and the Saudis were elated at receiving the tanks.

Negotiations for an extension to the airfield agreement remained bogged down, however. A major area of contention was continuing Saudi arms requests. These requests derived from a five-year military development plan (called the 1380 Plan), prepared with the help of USMTM but not formally accepted in Washington as a commitment to provide arms to the Kingdom. By May 1956, however, the United States had agreed to authorize the sale of all the items in the plan except M-47 medium tanks and F-86 fighter aircraft. Still the Saudis held out.

The other major sticking point in the negotiations was over money. The Saudis, as a matter of principle, thought that the United States ought to pay "rent"—in the form of a subsidy or grant aid—even though the bulk of the funds for the construction of the facility had been provided by the Americans in the first place. Although the United States was willing to provide grant aid or other financial assistance, it did not wish for tactical negotiating reasons to publicly link such aid with a military access agreement, nor did it wish such a subsidy to be out of line with the $44 million that the United States was paying Libya for the use of Wheelus Field.

The Saudis proved to be tough negotiators, even on issues where general agreement had been reached. U.S. negotiators, unused to the Middle East style of bargaining, often became frustrated—if not exasperated—over the Saudi propensity to haggle. In the end, however, most obstacles were surmounted to mutual satisfaction.

The general atmosphere in which negotiations were taking place began to improve by late 1956 as a result of U.S. opposition to the Israeli-British-French military action against Egypt in the Suez crisis. President Eisenhower had become convinced that Nasser would never make any move to settle outstanding differences with Israel after Egypt's shift to the Soviets. To counter Nasser's influence, Eisenhower even toyed briefly with the idea of building up King Saud's image as a conservative, spiritual leader.[13] In January-February 1957, King Saud visited Washington and expressed public support for the Eisenhower Doctrine, a move that set in train King Saud's final break with President Nasser.

The new Dhahran Air Field Agreement was finally concluded on April 22, 1957, in the form of an exchange of notes in Washington.[14] The agreement had no provision for cancellation prior to its expiration date. It extended U.S. access to Dhahran for a further period of five years.

As a quid pro quo, the United States agreed to provide grant military aid of up to $45 million over the period of the agreement for training (including army, navy, and air force) and for military construction incident to such training. Additionally, the United States agreed to provide $5 million for the construction of the Dhahran Civil Air Terminal and $20 million for the construction of a pier at the port of Dammam.[15] The United States also agreed to sell military equipment required for the two divisions proposed in the five-year plan, at a value of $110 million, and to provide $50 million in credit to enable the Kingdom to begin such purchases. Another U.S. concession on arms sales was the commitment to supply the Saudis with 116 tanks (of which the United States agreed immediately to sell 18 M-47s and 18 M-41s), ten propeller-driven training aircraft, eight T-33 aircraft, twelve F-86 aircraft, and two naval vessels.

Following the conclusion of the 1957 agreement, U.S.-Saudi military relations stabilized, but the relationship came under growing criticism from radical Arab states, making the airfield agreement an increasing liability to the Saudis. As King Saud distanced himself from President Nasser, the Egyptians became increasingly vociferous in their opposition to the Dhahran agreement, as did the Syrians, who joined with the Egyptians to form the United Arab Republic in 1958. In the previous year, King Saud had had a rapprochement with the Hashimite kings of Jordan and Iraq, but in 1958 the Iraqi monarchy was overthrown in a bloody coup by Abd al-Karim Qasim. Although Qasim became a rival of Nasser in intra-Arab politics, he did agree with the Egyptian president in his opposition to the U.S. military presence at Dhahran.

On the U.S. side, the value of the Dhahran airfield was also diminishing. Robert McNamara, secretary of defense in the new Kennedy administration, concluded that with the advent of intercontinental ballistic missiles, overseas Strategic Air Command (SAC) bases were no longer cost effective. Early in 1961, the Departments of State and Defense agreed to draft a joint U.S.-Saudi statement on nonrenewal, to be issued on March 18, 1961. King Saud, however, probably on the urging of his half-brother Prince Tallal bin Abd al-Aziz and apparently to reap domestic political capital, decided to make a unilateral announcement. In order to preempt the Saudis, the United States made a unilateral announcement on March 16, 1961. On April 2, 1962, the U.S. base rights at Dhahran formally came to an end, and with them came to an end a phase of U.S.-Saudi military relations that had begun almost two decades before. Nevertheless, the United States followed through in completing the Dhahran airport terminal, part of the original agreement.[16]

The Formative Years: 1962–1973

The cancellation of U.S. base rights in 1962 went far to reestablish U.S.-Saudi military relations on a firmer footing. Two other events occurred in that year that would improve relations even further. The first was the return of then Crown Prince Faysal to government after a two-year period of self-imposed retirement. In March 1962, he returned as vice prime minister, ending the mismanagement and court intrigue that characterized the rule of his brother, King Saud. In 1964, King Saud was forced to abdicate altogether in favor of Faysal.

Many of Faysal's 1962 cabinet appointments have remained in government, including the defense minister, Prince Sultan bin Abd al-Aziz, and the head of the National Guard, now Crown Prince Abdallah. Faysal also appointed the current king, Fahd, as interior minister at that time. This continuity in national security affairs has been a great asset to the Saudis in ongoing U.S.-Saudi relations, particularly in the formative years.

The second event affecting U.S.-Saudi military relations that occurred in 1962 was the outbreak of the Yemeni Civil War, which was to last until 1970. It created a security threat so serious to Saudi Arabia that, for the first time, the need to develop a modern, effective military force was seen by the Saudi leadership to outweigh the internal security risks inherent in creating such a force.

Since the 1930s when King Abd al-Aziz had disbanded his tribally based army, the Ikhwan (the Brethren), Saudi Arabia had remained one of the few countries in the Middle East in which the military played almost no political role. Signs of Nasserist-inspired unrest among the Saudi military during the stormy years of the 1950s and early 1960s had reinforced the regime's qualms over developing a modern armed force. These fears were further reinforced by the defection to Cairo of a number of Saudi air-force pilots early in the Yemen crisis.[17] In this context, USMTM was viewed as a physical symbol of the U.S. commitment to the defense of the regime. It was with considerable ambivalence, therefore, that the Saudis embarked on their first serious, comprehensive military modernization plans. Although they were to seek the aid of several countries in this venture—Britain, West Germany,

Pakistan, and France—they looked to the United States as their primary source of assistance.

The threat to Saudi internal security created by the Yemeni Civil War vividly brought home to the Saudis how far they had to go. Although by 1962 USMTM had been in the Kingdom for almost a decade, it had accomplished little. Not only were the Saudis not entirely committed to USMTM's success during its first ten years because of internal security reasons, but there was also a clear, if unarticulated, belief among the Saudi leadership that the United States was committed to defend the Kingdom should it be faced with a serious external threat.

The lack of positive results by USMTM was not solely a matter of Saudi qualms about the security risk of modernizing their armed forces. There was also the morale problem for U.S. advisors. Seeing few results from their efforts, they tended to lose their enthusiasm over their training role, particularly when they did not fully understand the broader political and psychological aspects of the U.S. military presence in the Kingdom. There were also administrative impediments. Most U.S. tours of duty were limited to one year, and personnel were unaccompanied by families. The Saudis consistently refused to fund two-year, accompanied tours primarily out of concern for the social impact of U.S. military families on the local society. (At that time, there were still fewer than one hundred westerners in all Riyadh, other than USMTM personnel.)

There were also legal and ethnic impediments. On the legal side, the United States wished to define more precisely the status of USMTM personnel and to make it easier to clear supplies through customs. On the ethnic side, the Kennedy administration objected to Paragraph 9 of the 1953 USMTM Agreement, which stipulated that Saudi Arabia would honor U.S. government travel documents in lieu of Saudi visas, "on condition that such persons are not undesirable to the Saudi Arabian Government."[18] The United States interpreted "undesirable" to refer to U.S. personnel of the Jewish faith and wanted new language that specifically disregarded race, religion, and color. Both the legal and ethnic questions, as is so often the case, were more symbolic than substantive, but they were among the issues subject to renegotiation of the agreement after the Dhahran airfield was closed in 1962. In part, the differences were cultural. The United States preferred such matters spelled out in detail whereas the Saudis felt that if sufficient trust, good will, and rapport existed on both sides, the details would take care of themselves. Negotiations dragged on through 1965 and were ultimately shelved with no appreciable loss to the operating efficiency of USMTM.

As befitting the growing importance of USMTM, the rank of its chief was raised from a colonel to a brigadier general, and after the closure of the Dhahran airfield it was shifted from an air force to an army officer billet. With the growing importance of the Saudi air defense system in the late 1970s, the job once again reverted to a U.S. Air Force officer, by then a major general.

In the mid-1960s, with manpower requirements in East Asia growing, the United States decided to cut the size of USMTM and other similar missions abroad. The move in Saudi Arabia was rationalized on grounds that USMTM's efficiency would not be impaired in view of a lack of Saudi receptiveness at the working level. This receptiveness declined even further as a result of the June 1967 Arab-Israeli war. The embassy in Jidda and USMTM correctly predicted that this reaction would be temporary and opposed the personnel cut, fearing that it would be interpreted by the Saudis as a symbol of disengagement. Nevertheless, by 1968, the mission staff was cut from 240 to 140.

The reduction was not viewed by the Kingdom as a sign of U.S. disengagement, however. A major reason why not was that, by this time, the Saudi armed forces had reached the stage where they had begun to launch new development plans and expand old ones, all involving U.S. civilian contract personnel. Indeed, by 1973, virtually all major Saudi military development programs involving the United States were in place.

The United States has used a variety of procedures over the years for providing arms, training, and other services to the Saudi military. Initially, most transfers were in the form of grant aid, offered as a quid pro quo for the use of the Dhahran airfield. On July 1, 1964, however, all grant aid was discontinued, with the exception of a few training billets reserved for Saudis in the United States and of the salaries of USMTM personnel (all other USMTM costs were and are still borne by the Saudis.)

A major grant aid item consisted of the twelve F-86 fighters the United States agreed to sell but then decided to "loan" to Saudi Arabia in 1957. Title to the F-86s was formally transferred to Saudi Arabia in 1964. Other Military Assistance Program (MAP) grants included two utility boats for the embryonic naval force. By the time grant aid was phased out in the mid-1960s, overall expenditure of MAP funds for Saudi Arabia was around $34 million.[19]

As grant aid ended, arms procurement shifted to government-to-government contracts, including Defense Department Foreign Military Sales (FMS) cases and direct sales of equipment and services by private contractors. In time, military sales grew to such a magnitude that commercial interests joined other U.S. political, economic, and strategic interests in helping to justify the military relationship with Saudi Arabia.

Rapidly expanding Saudi military programs after 1964 created additional problems in the negotiation and implementation of U.S. military sales. Between 1950 and 1964, total sales agreements amounted to $87 million, and deliveries were $75 million. In 1965 alone, agreements equaled $342 million; in 1974, the first year after the energy crisis, they exceeded $2 billion; and by 1980 total sales agreements equalled $35 billion, and deliveries were $11.3 billion.[20]

On the Saudi side, the growing magnitude of military transfers occasioned increasing sensitivity to price rises, delays in delivery schedules, and items not meeting specifications. In part, these resulted from the Saudis' own penchant for drawing out negotiations beyond the expiry date of letters of offer or authorization, which then themselves had to be renegotiated. Moreover, the Saudis would often also continue to negotiate for ancillary services once a base price had been agreed upon. Nevertheless, unilateral price rises did constitute a real problem for the Kingdom, which tended to treat an agreed-upon cost figure as inviolable.

Delivery schedules were an irritant, particularly during the Vietnam war period. The Saudi Defense Ministry understood that the priority of U.S. needs in Vietnam caused a delay in their deliveries, but the Saudis were nevertheless frustrated, particularly when, in their eyes, there did not appear to be a commensurate delay in U.S. deliveries to Israel. Damaged items and those not meeting specifications reinforced Saudi suspicions that Western arms suppliers often dumped "damaged" inferior arms on the Third World. The Saudis have never accepted the U.S. tolerance for a certain percentage of "duds" as a cost-saving measure. Moreover, issues of quality and suitability aside, the Saudis invariably demanded the best and latest model of whatever they ordered. On the other hand, the unique problems of military supply to a remote desert kingdom such as Saudi Arabia were not always fully appreciated back in the United States.

Political, commercial, and economic considerations also affected U.S. military programs in Saudi Arabia. One result was that the Saudis, particularly after the June 1967 Arab-Israeli war, made an effort to diversify the foreign sources for their defense requirements. These efforts incurred additional costs because of the difficulties of absorbing different and sometimes incompatible weapons systems into a single inventory. The extent to which the Saudis did—and continue to—incur such costs, therefore, can be used as an indicator of the state of U.S.-Saudi military relations at a given period of time.

Military sales to Saudi Arabia during the formative years, 1962–1973, were so competitive, and Saudi procurement procedures were so rudimentary, that vast sums changed hands in attempts by U.S. and other Western firms to influence the outcome of competitive bids. Such practices became the subject of intensive U.S. congressional hearings in the mid-1970s.[21] In part as a result of these congressional disclosures, the Saudis greatly tightened up their private-sector sales procedures and renewed their preference for government-to-government rather than government-to-industry procurement contracts.

U.S.–Saudi Arabian Military Programs

In early 1963, the Saudi Defense Ministry, working closely with USMTM, developed a comprehensive military reorganizational plan known as the Armed Forces Defense Plan No. 1. It provided for a gradual buildup of the Saudi Arabian army based on a modified U.S. brigade organizational structure, for creation of an organizational plan for the air force, and for development of a specific structure, purpose, and mission for the navy, then still a part of the army. Although the Armed Forces Defense Plan No. 1, like its predecessor, the 1380 Plan, was never formally adopted, it did become a general guide for Saudi and USMTM planning, reflecting the direction in military development that the Saudis wished to take. Subsequent U.S. military assistance programs, therefore, although they did not necessarily follow in a predetermined order, can be said to be lineal descendants of the recommendations and proposals embodied in the plan and not simply politically inspired U.S. responses to ad hoc Saudi arms requests, as they have often been characterized.

The Air Defense Program and the Creation of a Modern Saudi Air Force

The first major Saudi military expansion program begun during the formative years addressed the Kingdom's almost total lack of an air defense capability in the face of Egyptian bomb attacks emanating from the Yemeni Civil War. As early as 1961, Saudi Arabia had shown interest in acquiring supersonic fighter aircraft to augment its obsolescent F-86s. Despite British and French competition, the Saudis were particularly interested in the early model of the Northrop F-5, then in production. A major constraint to such an acquisition was the lack of air force organization addressed in Armed Forces Defense Plan No. 1.

The 1963 U.S. air defense survey for Saudi Arabia provided just that needed organizational planning. Originally offered by Ambassador Ellsworth Bunker as a sweetener to get King Faysal to sign a peace agreement with President Nasser over the Yemeni Civil War (see Chapter 5), this survey became the first blueprint for the creation of a Saudi air defense capability.

As an additional sweetener for concluding a Yemeni disengagement agreement, Bunker offered to send a fighter squadron to the Kingdom. This offer ultimately became known as Operation Hardsurface. It involved deployment of a squadron of U.S. Air Force (USAF) F-100s to Saudi Arabia on July 6, 1963, and lasted, with various extensions, until January 30, 1964. Although probably of limited strategic value, Operation Hardsurface did provide a psychological boost to U.S.-Saudi relations, which had reached a low ebb by the summer of 1963 over U.S. recognition of the Yemen Arab Republic and continuing Egyptian operations in that country.[22]

The U.S. air defense survey team, after a three-month study, completed a comprehensive air defense survey for Saudi Arabia in November 1963. A preliminary report was presented to the Saudi defense minister, Prince Sultan, on December 23, and the full report was submitted to the Saudis on January 20, 1964. The survey called for acquisition of surface-to-air (SAM) missiles, an air defense radar net, and three squadrons of twelve supersonic aircraft each, either the Northrop F-5 or the Lockheed F-104.

The U.S. government professed no preference between the two aircraft, and stiff competition very quickly developed between the manufacturers. Northrop had hired Kermit Roosevelt, a well-connected former Central Intelligence Agency (CIA) official, to represent its interests in Saudi Arabia.[23] Lockheed hired Adnan Khashoggi, a young Saudi businessman of Turkish origins who was soon to become infamous for his dealings not only with Lockheed but with other U.S. arms manufacturers as well.[24]

At that point, events were happening elsewhere that were to negate the efforts of both companies. In 1965, Britain was again undergoing a severe balance-of-payments crisis, placing in jeopardy its ability to purchase F-111 aircraft from the United States. In an effort to bring about the sale, the U.S. defense secretary, Robert McNamara, worked out an arrangement with the British air minister, Roy Jenkins, whereby the United States would facilitate British military exports of $400 million. Specifically, it was agreed that the United States would not strenuously contest British participation in a joint U.S.–United Kingdom air defense package to Saudi Arabia in which the British would supply three squadrons of F-52 Lightning aircraft, an air defense center, five sector operations centers plus associated early warning radar and communications equipment, and a five-year maintenance and training program. The total cost was estimated at between $275 million and $400 million.[25] The United States, for its part of the package, would supply 150 Raytheon Hawk surface-to-air missiles for ten batteries (six launches per battery), at a cost of $126 million.[26]

Although the United States never formally withdrew its offer of F-5s or F-104s, the Saudis clearly received the impression that Washington favored the joint package. British Defense Minister Denis Healey later stated that the Americans backed the United Kingdom proposal, but had told the British that they could not formally withdraw an all-U.S. offer looked upon favorably by the Saudis. In announcing the sale to Parliament in December 1965, John Stonehouse, parliamentary secretary to the Air Ministry, admitted that it could not have been made without "American cooperation."[27]

The commercial aspects of the British deal were allowed to be transacted by a private businessman from Yorkshire, Geoffrey Edwards. He had been trying to put together a similar British arms package for the Saudis since the early 1960s. The final contracts, for which Edwards was amply rewarded, were with British Aircraft Corporation (BAC) for the Lightnings; with Allied Electronics Industries, Limited, for the early warning radar system; and with Airwork Services, Limited, which was created to provide training and maintenance. The Saudis signed the Raytheon contract on May 4, 1966, and signed a contract with BAC for 40 Lightnings, 25 Prevost jet trainers, and 8 Cessna 172 (CT-41) trainers on the following day. In 1968, a $52 million add on was negotiated with Raytheon for an additional half battery of Hawk missiles for training and other construction and services; and in 1973, the United States agreed to the Saudi purchase of improved Hawks (I-Hawks). An I-Hawk contract was signed with Raytheon in April 1978.[28]

In addition to these sales, the air defense package included government-to-government sale of U.S. Sidewinder air-to-air missiles for the F-86 squadron. The U.S. Middle East arms embargo delayed the sale, but early in 1968 a letter of offer was signed for one hundred AIM-9E missiles and modification kits for the F-86s. In the spring of 1969, the Saudis also acquired eight T-33 jet trainers from the United States.

The British part of the package was never very successful. The Saudis were not pleased with the performance of Airwork or the equipment from BAC and AEI. The radars had never been proven under operational conditions prior to the sale, and the Lightnings, designed for short-range combat over Britain, were singularly ill suited for extended combat patrols over the vast desert reaches of Saudi Arabia. The ultimate irony, however, was that in November 1967 Britain encountered yet another economic crisis and cancelled the F-111 purchase. As one writer on the debate stated it, "The Saudis in the end had been persuaded to buy British planes they did not want, to allow Britain to pay for American planes they could not afford."[29]

The delays in negotiations and the recognition that at least several years would pass before the air defense system would be operational induced the Saudis to purchase an "instant" air defense capability for the southern sector of the Kingdom bordering Yemen. In March 1966, the Saudi Ministry of Defense and Aviation signed a separate contract with Airwork called Operation Magic Carpet. In it, Airwork contracted to provide 6 Lightnings, 6 Hawker Hunter aircraft, 12 contract pilots, 2 Mark 7 radars and a 424 radar, 2 British Thunderbird surface-to-air batteries (one for training), and personnel to maintain and operate all the equipment.[30] The Saudis were equally dissatisfied with Airwork's performance of Magic Carpet, and when the contract expired in March 1968, they negotiated a government-to-government contract with Pakistan for its maintenance and operation, although Airwork still provided pilots.

Despite successes of the Lightnings and F-86s in beating off an attack on the southern border post at al-Wadiy'ah in November 1969, the Saudis were already considering the replacement of both. To replace the F-86s, the Saudis settled on Northrop's F-5s, somewhat of a turn around as they seemed to be leaning toward the F-104s prior to the Lightning sale. Prince Sultan, however, appeared to have been impressed with the F-5s' performance in Vietnam.

On May 29, 1971, a formal request was made to purchase 20 F-5As (and F-5B trainers), together with necessary equipment, spare parts, training components for Saudi pilots, and training personnel. On September 29, Prince Sultan signed a $106.7 million letter of offer. Wary of government-to-industry contracts, apparently because of growing publicity about previous contracts and out of a desire to involve the U.S. government in helping to oversee the contract, he insisted it be government-to-government. The subsequent revelation in congressional hearings of questionable Northrop payments to its Saudi agent, Adnan Khashoggi, and to others is all the more interesting in light of the government-to-government sale. It does suggest that Khashoggi probably had less influence on the sale than either he claimed or than Northrop apparently believed. The publicity attached to charges of corruption aired during the congressional hearings, however, had a very adverse effect on the atmosphere within which U.S.-Saudi military relations were conducted over the next several years.[31]

In contrast to some earlier foreign military sales, the United States was highly enthusiastic about the F-5 sale. Although not in the USAF inventory, it had been designated an "export fighter," specifically designed for sale to friendly Third World countries as an inexpensive, simple, but quality fighter. Saudi Arabia, moreover, was subsequently the first purchaser of the more advanced F-5E and its trainer version, the F-5F.

A second al-Wadiy'ah incident involving a South Yemeni MIG-17 attack occurred on March 22, 1973; several Saudis were wounded at this time. The delivered Saudi F-5s still lacked most of the armaments originally agreed upon in 1971, particularly air-to-ground missiles. Fearing the incident might presage a larger South Yemeni attack, King Faysal asked for and received an accelerated delivery of F-5 ordnance, a factor that helped to restore better U.S.-Saudi military relations. To replace the Lightnings, still their front-line fighter, the Saudis as early as 1969 had begun to consider the F-4 Phantom. Even though in May 1973 they signed a new five-year contract with BAC for maintenance of the Lightnings, the Saudis had received in the same month a U.S. approval in principle to purchase F-4s. The agreement, however, provoked strong official Israeli concern when news of the decision broke in the press. In response, the State Department issued a policy statement saying that any military sales to Iran, Saudi Arabia, or Kuwait would take "fully into account our longstanding policy of support for Israeli security."[32]

In September 1973, a USAF team briefed Prince Sultan on the Phantom. Within days, however, the October 1973 Arab-Israeli war broke out, and Saudi interest in the F-4 waned. It did not take much imagination, however, to conclude that the Saudis would be taking a hard look at the next generation of U.S. fighters to replace their aging Lightnings.

Despite so much attention being placed on air defense during this period, a more modest but very successful program was being administered by Lockheed to provide the Saudis with a military air transport capability. In 1965, the Saudis bought four Lockheed C-130 transport aircraft. Lockheed was also given a management-training contract. The Saudi Ministry of Defense and Aviation was so pleased with the performance of the C-130s and with Lockheed that it negotiated the sale of an additional aircraft in 1966, paying for it with the proceeds of the sale to the United States of five older C-123 transports and spare parts acquired in the late 1950s through private commercial channels. By 1969, the Saudis had purchased eight C-130s, deployed in two transport squadrons. The C-130s gave Saudi Arabia its first real airlift capability, an important development in a large, sparsely populated country.

The U.S. role in the development of the Royal Saudi Air Force and air defense capability during the formative years, 1962–1973, had its share of problems: redundancies, inefficiencies, commercial irregularities, and false starts. Nevertheless, it produced, on balance, a positive record of achievement and a real basis for the further expansion that was to occur in the 1970s and 1980s. Given the limited ability of the Saudi military to absorb new expansion programs, the record of achievement was all the more impressive. It was a record on which both the United States and Saudi Arabia could look back with pride.

Role of the U.S. Army Corps of Engineers

The Corps of Engineers (COE) has played an almost unique role in the development of the Saudi armed forces. A great deal of its success resulted from the trust in its advice and performance held by the Saudis, particularly the late King Faysal. In many ways, this trust extended COE activities into areas that could have been served by private consulting engineering firms. A 1973 American Embassy briefing paper expressed the dilemma for U.S. policy in wishing to be responsive to Saudi requests while at the same time trying to keep COE activities within acceptable limits. "The COE," it stated, "is not seeking new projects, though it will inevitably have to assume additional projects during the life of this agreement."[33] The document referred to was the Agreement for the Construction of Military Facilities, which became effective on May 24, 1965.[34]

As early as March 1964, the Saudi Defense Ministry had shown interest in the availability of the COE for military construction as well as for a study of automotive requirements for the Saudi armed forces. In May 1964, a COE team arrived in the Kingdom for preliminary discussions, and in June a three-man COE office was established. By 1973, the COE mission had grown to a staff of ninety-seven[35] and was to expand further throughout the 1970s. The primary construction projects during this period were the military cantonment at Khamis Mushayt, completed in 1971, and the one at Tabuk, finished the following year. By 1973, initial site surveys were underway for a third cantonment at Qaysumah (Hafr al-Batin), and discussions were under way for construction of a new Ministry of Defense and Aviation headquarters, for a Saudi military academy in Riyadh, for new National Guard facilities, and for Saudi naval bases at Jubayl on the Gulf and Jidda on the Red Sea.[36]

The COE was also involved in a number of programs not directly related to military construction. One was to supervise the construction and management of a television network, a project that actually predated the military construction agreement. The original Agreement for the Establishment of a Television System in Saudi Arabia was effected by an exchange of notes on December 9, 1963, and January 6, 1964. It was amended by an exchange of notes on May 23 and 27, 1967, for the construction of a radio facility complex.[37] The private contractor was originally National Broadcasting Corporation (NBC) and then AVCO. The agreement expired in August 1973.

Two other COE-supervised projects involved the Saudi army. Defense Minister Prince Sultan's original interest in COE assistance in upgrading the army's mobility resulted in the Saudi Arabian Mobility Program (SAMP), agreed upon on September 7, 1966. The agreement provided for COE to supervise a five-year, $120 million program. It included the purchase of 4,276 general and special purpose vehicles and spare parts, the providing of maintenance services, an automated supply system, and training of Saudi personnel in maintenance, and supply skills. A private contractor, Commonwealth-Tumpane, was hired by the Saudis to operate and maintain the program.

The task facing Commonwealth-Tumpane and the COE was enormous. The Saudi army did not have an inventory of its own rolling stock, and its procurement was highly decentralized, utilizing local suppliers. This situation not only invited irregular practices, but the purchase of many models and makes of vehicle (two 1938 Humber halftracks were allegedly found in an al-Kharj warehouse) precluded even the most rudimentary standardization. Moreover, many Saudi commanders initially regarded SAMP as an open-ended arrangement under which any vehicle could be repaired on order, regardless of vintage, origin, or condition.

On October 17, 1967, a $9.9 million add-on program called the Armaments Repair and Maintenance Program (RAMP) was concluded between Secretary McNamara and Prince Sultan. It called for the development of a plan for supply and maintenance management of vehicles, small arms, tanks, and artillery; procurement of tools, equipment, and spare parts needed for maintenance and repair; introduction of standards of repair and maintenance based on the U.S. Army logistics system; and the construction of maintenance, repair, and training facilities.[38] The reasonably successful SAMP/RAMP program was phased out in 1972. Thereafter, COE undertook in a separate memorandum of understanding to work with the newly organized Saudi Arabian Army Ordnance Corps in supervising another private contractor, Bendix-Syanco, which undertook to continue management of the Saudi army's repair and maintenance program.[39]

The expansion of COE activities raised a new bureaucratic issue for the United States in Saudi Arabia. The COE office was originally a part of the Mediterranean Division in Livorno, Italy, set up at the end of World War II to help reconstruct Europe. As European projects were terminated, so was the division, and in the 1970s, the Saudi office was raised to a division headed by a general officer. Anticipating the need to delineate the areas of responsibility between COE and USMTM, an agreement for in-country coordination was negotiated between the two organizations by Ambassador Hermann Eilts and signed on January 7, 1967. Writing to Washington, Eilts observed, "It is not the text of the Agreement which is important, but the spirit of cooperation which the two military missions demonstrate when working on problems of mutual concern."[40] This spirit of cooperation became particularly important in the 1970s with the great expansion of U.S. military programs to the kingdom.

The Saudi Naval Expansion Program

The Royal Saudi Naval Force was formally established in 1957 as an adjunct of the army. By the early 1960s, it still lacked a formalized mission, a planned composition, or a development plan. Not until 1963 did a naval officer replace an army officer as its commander, and not until 1969 did it begin functioning as a separate military service. In the interim, however, plans for the ultimate development of the navy did begin to materialize. In 1964, an organizational plan recommended either building a naval base or else upgrading the Coast Guard pier at Dammam into a naval base. At the time, naval craft used the Ministry of Transportation pier at Dammam and later began sharing the Coast Guard pier.

By 1966, the Saudi Ministry of Defense and Aviation had begun to consider two naval bases, one on the Gulf and the other on the Red Sea. In April 1968, Prince Sultan formally asked for U.S. assistance. In the meantime, he had apparently asked the British, French, and Pakistanis for similar studies. The British in particular wished to assist,[41] probably motivated more by commercial reason than by any desire to replace USMTM. One item the British would certainly have liked to have unloaded at the time was an unwanted ship, originally ordered by Ghana and called Nkrumah's Folly. The Saudis, however, did not want it either.

From August 1968 to February 1969, a three-man U.S. naval team made a complete survey of Saudi naval needs. They ultimately recommended an operational base at Jidda, an operational and training base at Jubayl, and a headquarters facility at Riyadh. In order to ease endemic Saudi manpower problems, the team recommended that maintenance and repair be done by contract personnel and that a ten-year program be adopted envisioning two flotillas (one for each coast for a total of twelve vessels). King Faysal felt that twelve vessels were not sufficient for the protection of such large stretches of coastline, and the Ministry of Defense thereupon made a counterproposal for a twenty-five–ship navy. After further study, a compromise goal of a nineteen-ship navy was agreed upon by a joint Saudi-U.S. team in November 1971. The result was the Saudi Arabian Naval Expansion Plan (SNEP), which came into being in January 1972.[42] It called for four 700-ton guided missile patrol boats, nine 300-ton guided missile patrol boats, four MSC-322 coastal minecraft, and eight smaller craft. Overall direction of SNEP was assigned to USMTM, and supervision of base and facility construction was assigned to the Corps of Engineers.

The Saudi Arabian National Guard Modernization Program

The National Guard was formed in 1956 from remnants of the old tribal army known as the Ikhwan, with which King Abd al-Aziz reunited the country in the early decades of this century. The Ikhwan had been more or less disbanded in the mid-1930s. From the beginning, the guard was recruited through levies on tribes loyal to the Al Saud (the royal family); in the 1950s and 1960s, it was seen as a counterbalance to the regular armed forces in a period of rising revolution throughout the Middle East. In addition, it originally played an important role as a conduit to distribute subsidies to the proud but needy tribesmen afflicted by a sustained period of drought that had devastated their way of nomadic life. Because of the flowing white robes, or thaubs, worn by the guard, they were popularly known as the White Army.

During the rule of King Saud, the guard was administered directly from the palace under a succession of the king's sons aided by a small civilian staff. When Crown Prince (later King) Faysal returned to power as prime minister in 1962, he appointed his half-brother Abdallah to be the new commander. Thus Prince Abdallah became the "father" of the modern National Guard as his half-brother Prince Sultan became the "father" of the modern armed forces. Not only did the guard represent inter alia a check on the regular army, but as the two half-brothers represented different sibling groups within the royal family, the distinction between the guard and the regular armed forces had broader political implications as well.

Almost immediately upon his appointment as commander, Abdallah began to reorganize and modernize the National Guard. Some new equipment was purchased, and an ex-Syrian police colonel was brought in as an advisor. The few relatively trained guardsmen, called commandos, or *fida'iyin,* were reorganized into two regular units (*firqas*) of one thousand men each. A third *firqa* was raised in 1963, the officers being drawn almost entirely from Saudis from the northern tribes with long service in the neighboring Jordanian Arab Legion. The rest of the guard was placed in about twenty-eight irregular units, called *liwa's.* In 1963, Prince Abdallah turned to the British to establish an advisory mission headed by a Brigadier Timbrell. In 1963, he was replaced by Brigadier Roy Watson, who was succeeded by Nigel Brummage, followed by Adrian Donaldson. Also recruited were some senior British-trained Jordanian officers, including General Ibrahim Husayni. Throughout the rest of the 1960s, the British mission sought to convert the guard into a modern, paramilitary force.

During this period, the guard earned its keep on at least two occasions. When King Saud was forced to abdicate in 1964, he still had the support of some two thousand personal retainers and the half-support of the Royal Guard (since abolished). The National Guard stood down Saud's supporters without a shot being fired, thus playing a key role in the peaceful accession of Faysal as king. The other occasion occurred during the June 1967 Arab-Israeli war. Riots and demonstrations broke out in the Eastern Province, doing damage to the Aramco compound, the American Consulate General, and the USMTM quarters at the Dhahran airfield. Before the disturbances could spread, the guard was called in and quickly dispersed the rioters.

In 1965, Prince Abdallah turned to the United States for the first time to purchase weapons. Two FMS cases were drawn up for 81-mm mortars, 90-mm recoilless rifles, and 50-caliber machine guns worth about $7 million. Because of the politics and personalities involved, it was thought better to handle the sale through the office of the U.S. defense attaché at the American Embassy rather than through USMTM, so closely involved with the regular armed forces. Despite many problems with the sale, including a delay in delivery due to a brief U.S. arms embargo to the Middle East following the 1967 Arab-Israeli war, the diligence and personal charm of the army attaché, Lieutenant Colonel James Broady, helped make the sale a success.[43]

By the end of the 1960s, Prince Abdallah began to look increasingly toward the Americans for assistance, despite the American Embassy's assurance that the United States had no desire to replace the British, who in its view had done an excellent job. Nevertheless, in September 1971, Abdallah asked for assistance in modernizing the guard along the lines of a report prepared by the British mission. After some hesitation, the United States agreed to survey guard needs. Due to some incompatibility between British and U.S. organizational concepts and equipment, the survey ended up as a totally new one. The study led to a detailed modernization plan on the basis of which the United States agreed to train and equip four *firqas*. The Saudi Arabian National Guard Program (SANG) was established in March 1973.[44] The program was assigned to the U.S. Army Materiel Development Command with COE to supervise design and construction of all guard facilities.

The Leahy Report

One other U.S. military assistance effort during the formative years is worthy of mention. As Saudi military modernization began to advance in all branches of the armed services and the National Guard, competition for scarce manpower resources among the branches and between them and the private sector became intense. A standard Saudi response to manpower shortages was to insist on a training component for each program. However, the real problem was not training, but finding available personnel to train. As early as 1969, the Americans began considering the efficacy of offering to the Saudis another comprehensive military development plan, such as the O'Keefe report and the Armed Forces Defense Plan No. 1, to consider needs and resources of all Saudi uniformed services. In January 1970, Prince Sultan requested such a study, and Major General Oswald Leahy conducted it. As with its predecessors, the study was never formally adopted by the Saudis, but it did become a guide for future planning in the 1970s. One of the rationales of the study accepted by the Saudis and used in future requests for more sophisticated weapons systems was that, due to severe manpower constraints, the Saudis needed to develop a capital-intensive rather than a labor-intensive military establishment.

The Post–Energy Crisis Years: 1973–1978

By 1973, virtually every major ongoing military development project that the United States has undertaken or is still undertaking was in place. The only security force in which there has been no U.S. assistance program is the Saudi Coast Guard and Frontier Force, and in the late 1960s there was some thought given to that. Even the Saudi national police force was the recipient in the late 1960s of a technical services program developed by the United States Agency for International Development to improve capabilities in forensic science and communications (including the use of mobile single-sideband radios). On balance, a solid record of military cooperation developed during this period between the two countries. This cooperation has become the underlying basis of subsequent arms requests despite increasing political sensitivity.

In some ways, the foundations of the post-1973 period actually were laid in 1968 when the British announced their intention to end their protective status with the Arab states of the lower Gulf by 1971. For both the United States and Saudi Arabia, this announcement was met with a certain amount of concern. The previous year, the British had departed Aden, leaving newly independent South Yemen in the hands of a Marxist regime. In the neighboring Dhufar province of Oman, South Yemen had immediately begun aiding fellow Marxists leading a rebellion against the Omani government.[45] In the north, hostility between Iraq and Iran was building up in a characteristically cyclical fashion. Moreover, in 1969 and 1970, the Saudis uncovered an antigovernment plot that resulted in the arrest of a number of military officers and civilians and added to Saudi security concerns.

The United States, in particular, began to view security in the Gulf and in the Indian Ocean separately from its traditional Middle East focus on the eastern Mediterranean and the Northern Tier states of Turkey, Iran, and Pakistan, all bordering on the Soviet Union. In Washington's new focus on the Gulf, Saudi Arabia became not merely a peripheral strategic concern but a central concern in what was to evolve into a U.S. Persian Gulf strategy.

The energy crisis of 1973 added a further dimension to U.S. strategic concern for Gulf—and particularly Saudi Arabian—security. The oil shortage of that period brought home to Washington the vital importance of Gulf oil to the free world and the vulnerability of the Gulf oil fields to both conventional attack and acts of sabotage.

The United States was in no position to replace the British in the Gulf due to the isolationist mood at home in the wake of the Vietnam War. As a result, a Gulf policy was developed based on the Nixon Doctrine, a policy the president announced in 1969 that called for the United States to assist in the buildup of the strong regional allies that would obviate the need to station U.S. troops abroad. The new Gulf policy, called the Two Pillar Policy, looked to Iran and Saudi Arabia as the two regional powers that, it was hoped, could fill the so-called power vacuum left by the departure of the British. Iran, with roughly ten times the population of Saudi Arabia, logically came to be seen as the stronger pillar. This disparity somewhat inhibited Iranian-Saudi cooperation, already split by ethnic, confessional, and nationalistic rivalries. Nevertheless, the Two Pillar Policy was relatively successful, at least in the context of Gulf security, until the fall of the shah of Iran in 1979, and it provided a backdrop for U.S.-Saudi military relations during that period.

Commercial and political incentives were also involved in the Two Pillar Policy. The quantum jump in Saudi military expenditures was seen in the United States as a beneficial method of "recycling petro-dollars." The political imperative of maintaining good relations with the newly emerged oil giant also overlapped into the military sphere. It was reflected most clearly in the increased U.S. desire to be responsive to Saudi arms and military assistance requests, even in instances in which the United States had doubts about the cost effectiveness of a given request.

Saudi military development programs expanded rapidly during the 1970s. Money was no longer a constraint, and costs escalated. USMTM again grew in size, reaching 250 by the mid-1970s, and was further augmented by Training Assistance Field Teams (TAFTs). One of the most notable areas of increased U.S.-Saudi military cooperation was in air defense. With a number of younger-generation Saudi princes taking pilot training, the Saudi air force quickly became the glamour service branch. By 1975, USMTM's planning efforts had been upgraded to a comprehensive air defense development plan called Peace Hawk.[46] At the same time, the Saudis had purchased thirty more F-5Es and had one hundred more on order.[47] The working relationship between the Royal Saudi Air Force and the prime contractor, Northrop, had also greatly improved into a smoothly running partnership. In March 1976,

Northrop received a maintenance and service contract for the Peace Hawk program worth a reported $1.5 billion.[48] Between 1976 and 1980, Northrop's sales to Saudi Arabia averaged over $1.2 billion, 22 to 44 percent of its total sales.[49]

The Saudi navy and National Guard programs also came into full operation during this period. Cost escalations were particularly steep in SNEP. From original estimates of $180 million, costs had reached $2 billion by 1977,[50] even though in 1974 the expansion was scaled down to a less ambitious level. On the Saudi side, the problem was mainly a shortage of manpower. On the U.S. side, the U.S. Navy had had far less experience in managing foreign military programs than had the other service branches and took somewhat longer, therefore, to smooth out some of the original delays. In May 1979, a U.S. firm, HBH (a creation of Hughes Aircraft, Bendix Corporation, and Holmes and Narver), acquired a $671 million operation and management contract for the program. In the meantime, the COE-supervised construction of the naval bases at Jidda and Jubayl, the headquarters at Riyadh, and the repair facility at Dammam proceeded ahead of schedule, with the formal opening at Jubayl occurring in 1980. Naval construction was to continue well into the 1980s at a cost of about $2.5 billion.[51]

Despite the initial memorandum of understanding for the development of the National Guard in 1973, negotiations continued two more years. King Faysal himself questioned whether Abdallah should sign the memorandum of understanding, but the latter took the position that it was merely the key in the engine, which if turned on would permit the program to move ahead. Part of the delay was due to the outbreak of the October 1973 Arab-Israeli war. More important, however, was an early difference over the nature of the contract, which had already delayed the signing of the 1973 agreement for two years. The U.S. government, already directly involved in so many military projects in the kingdom, wished to avoid a direct supervisory role with the guard, particularly as it would involve creating a second military advisory mission independent of USMTM. Thus the United States recommended a direct government-to-industry contract. The Saudis appreciated the advantage of a commercial contract, and Abdallah had already been talking to Raytheon about an operation and management contract. The king, however, was becoming increasingly sensitive to charges of corruption in defense procurement and had developed a stated preference for government-to-government agreements as a way to circumvent Saudi commercial middlemen. Such contracts would also oblige the contracting government to oversee the activities of the private contractor, a desire the Saudis developed out of their experience with the Airwork contract back in the 1960s.

The 1973 agreement did involve the U.S. Army directly in a supervisory capacity with a separate mission. By 1975, however, the Saudis finally agreed to let a commercial contract to a private U.S. firm. Ironically, Raytheon did not get the contract. Despite official U.S. support, King Faysal was apparently adamant that Raytheon should not be considered because of its association with Adnan Khashoggi and others.[52] Instead the contract went to the Vinel Corporation of Anaheim, California.

The original U.S. commitment to the National Guard involved modernization of two mechanized infantry battalions (*firqas*) and two artillery batteries at an estimated cost of $200 million over four years. The program was expanded to include four infantry *firqas* and one supporting artillery battalion, to be developed over five and one-half years. The infantry battalions were to receive Cadillac-Gauge V-150 Commando armored cars, 20-mm cannon, tube-launched optically tracked wire-guided (TOW) antitank guided missiles, and other arms, and the artillery battalion was to be equipped with 105-mm M-102 howitzers and Vulcan 20-mm multiple-barrel air defense weapons. In addition, COE was to supervise design and construction of a multimillion-dollar National Guard headquarters and an academy in Riyadh. The U.S. army mission overseeing the SANG program grew to include seventy-five military personnel headed by a brigadier general.[53]

U.S. assistance to the Saudi army took a lower profile during the 1970s. This was in part because the air force became the prestige service, and the navy had so far to go in its development. Moreover, the Saudi army, more than any other service, tailored its development to multiple-country equipment purchases. In 1973, the Saudis began to buy French arms, including AMX-30 tanks, and at the same time U.S. arms, including M-60 tanks. The army thus became divided into two distinct groups, one predominantly French equipped and the other U.S. equipped. The strength of the army development program was its conservatism, concentrating on infrastructure and training and seeking to avoid overrapid expansion and overpurchase of weaponry. The disadvantage was the virtual necessity of two separate supply and logistic systems in a force already beset with manpower problems. The problem was exacerbated by subsequent purchase of British arms.[54]

As might be expected, a certain degree of competitive élan arose between the French- and U.S.-equipped units. The French-trained units, with greater contract assistance, developed somewhat faster, but the U.S. advisors, with their more heuristic approach to training, maintained that in time of emergency, with foreign personnel removed, the units they trained had developed more self-reliance, particularly at the unit level.[55]

The irony of the Two Pillar Policy was that by attempting to obviate the need for direct U.S. military involvement in Gulf security, it quickly gave rise to criticism in the U.S. Congress and elsewhere that U.S. arms sales to Iran and Saudi Arabia were creating an arms race. Although a true arms race is generally between antagonists, and Saudi Arabia and Iran despite their differences were generally considered allies, the concept of a Saudi-Iranian arms race nevertheless began to gain acceptance in the United States by 1974, often among the same critics who had worried about a Gulf power vacuum only a few years before. A less articulated Iran-Iraq arms race was also mentioned at the time, with what turned out to be prophetic accuracy, but the differences between Iran and Iraq were and are far too complex to be relegated to the single concept of an arms race.

The most obvious factor lending credence to the so-called arms race was the quantum jump in defense spending by Iran and Saudi Arabia following the quadrupling of oil prices in 1973. In 1973, total Saudi defense expenditures were around $2.8 billion, and Iranian expenditures were about $3.7 billion. Saudi defense spending increased to $7.1 billion in 1975, $9.3 billion in 1976, and $10.2 billion in 1978. Iranian spending jumped to $8.6 billion in 1976, $9.5 billion in 1976, and $10.6 billion in 1978.[56]

Although total Saudi and Iranian defense spending was roughly equal, Saudi spending on arms was in fact much less, accounting for only around 20 percent of total Saudi military expenditures, compared to a little less than one-third of Iranian military expenditures. The other 80 percent of Saudi military expenditures went into infrastructure and construction projects.[57] This fact, however, was ignored in virtually all the congressional testimony opposing arms sales during this period.[58] Another factor ignored was that the Saudi military purchases were based for the most part not on their own projections of needs but on studies, surveys, and recommendations of U.S. military teams and advisors, extending all the way back to the O'Keefe report of 1949. Congressional criticism of requests developed from U.S. recommendations thus set the stage for a renewed ambivalence in U.S.-Saudi military relations that was to follow the fall of the shah.

Congressional scrutiny of Saudi purchase requests also involved questioning Saudi motives for purchases, including stockpiling arms to be used by other Arab states against Israel (assuming the Saudis could not use them themselves).[59] This scrutiny increased following the energy crisis of 1973-1974. Saudi Arabia, despite its still minuscule military capability, came to be considered a strategic threat to Israel by Israel's supporters in the United States. In point of fact, the "threat" was probably seen more in terms of oil power and its effects on U.S.–Middle

East policies than in terms of Saudi military power, but this did not in any way lessen the public debate in the United States over military sales to Saudi Arabia.

Other factors in the debate over military sales to the kingdom involved corruption and waste. Corruption was dealt with exhaustively in the congressional hearings on multinational corporations.[60] Other criticism was leveled at what by Western standards were considered gross examples of waste. The army base being constructed at Hafr al-Batin, King Khalid Military City, for example, is expected to cost over $8.5 billion by the time it is completed in the mid-1980s.[61] There is no doubt that the Saudi penchant for "gold-plated" appointments and the most advanced model weapons systems resulted in expenditures that could not be justified by Western cost-accounting standards, nor even on occasion by Saudi standards. Nevertheless, those two sets of standards are different. With huge foreign-exchange balances and rudimentary military infrastructure, the marginal utility of the last riyal was considerably low. Moreover, there was a security consideration involved in terms of maintaining the loyalty of the military. Lavish appointments were consciously acquired by the Saudis to compensate its military establishment for the comparative lack of business opportunities available in the private sector. Finally, spending was one way to divert public funds to the private sector, a major task for the oil-rich government. Thus, while examples of waste certainly did exist, outside critics seldom portrayed it in the context of the Saudis' priorities for allocation of their resources.

Crises and Litmus Tests of Friendship: 1978–1981

U.S.-Saudi military relations again entered a period of ambivalence after 1978, in large part the result of four crises: the fall of the shah and the eruption of hostilities between Marxists in South Yemen and North Yemen, both in early 1979; the Soviet invasion of Afghanistan in late 1979; and the Iran-Iraq war, which broke out in 1980. Additional differences arose over the singling out of Saudi Arabia by friends of Israel as a major confrontation state facing Israel, particularly after the Saudis refused to accede to the Camp David Accords, and over differences in U.S. and Saudi public perceptions over the role of the Kingdom in OPEC, whether a moderating one or one designed to squeeze the oil-consuming West for every dollar a barrel of oil could bring.

During this period, U.S.-Saudi relations focused on two arms requests that came to be regarded by the Saudis as "litmus tests" of friendship: the F-15 request in 1978 and the air defense "enhancement package" of 1981. The latter centered around the Saudi request for airborne warning and control system (AWACS) aircraft. Both arms requests were granted, but not without stiff congressional opposition that itself had as negative an influence on the state of U.S.-Saudi military relations as the U.S. government's willingness to make the sales had a positive influence.

When the F-15 request was submitted to the Congress for approval in the spring of 1978, opponents of the sale sought to give the impression that it was an ad hoc request made for primarily political reasons, having little military logic or justification in light of the limited capabilities of the Saudi air force. In fact, when the Saudis abandoned the idea of purchasing F-4s back in 1973, it was a virtual certainty that, unless political considerations dictated that they purchase aircraft elsewhere, it would be only a matter of time before they would request the sale of one of the next generation of U.S. fighters: F-14s, F-15s, F-16s, or F-18s. In 1974, in the aftermath of the Saudi-led oil embargo, the United States dispatched a team that recommended replacing the aged Lightnings with an advanced fighter. The following year the Saudis sent a team to evaluate the new generation of U.S. aircraft. The Saudis selected the F-15, which was also fairly predictable. The F-15 was the most logical choice for Saudi needs: It had two engines (which they wanted), was less complicated than the F-14, and had more potential for upgrading than the F-16.

On the U.S. side, the F-15 was also seen as a good choice. The Saudi purchase would lower the unit cost for U.S. F-15s. Moreover, the sale of F-15s, which were primarily air superiority fighters, was considered easier to defend against anticipated congressional charges that it was a threat to Israel than the sale of F-16s, which were primarily attack fighters. Thus, the Ford administration approved the proposed sale of sixty F-15s provided no action be taken until after the 1976 presidential election.[62]

The incoming Carter administration reaffirmed the U.S. commitment and set out to obtain congressional approval. Among other things, the Carter administration sought to overcome opponents by promising fifteen more F-15s to Israel to "compensate" for the Saudi sale (thus linking U.S. arms sales to Israel with those to Saudi Arabia). The Carter administration also insured superiority of the Israeli F-15s over the Saudi version by omitting crucial avionics in the Saudi F-15s and by also eliminating "hard spots" in the air frame, making future upgrading for an attack mission virtually impossible.[63]

These well-publicized assurances that the sale would not upset the Middle East military balance (that is, Israeli preponderance) failed to reassure Israel and its U.S. supporters and only served to irritate Saudi Arabia. The Israeli supporters mounted an unprecedented campaign to win congressional disapproval of the sale.[64] Leading arguments against the sale aimed more at an emotional than an analytical response. For example, they took contradictory lines of reasoning. On the one hand, the Saudi air force was portrayed as so embryonic that it could not possibly absorb the then most advanced fighter in the world. On the other hand, it was argued that upon acquisition of such aircraft, the Saudi air force would constitute such a threat to Israel that, in case of another Arab-Israeli war, Israel would have to entertain the option of preemptive retaliation.[65] As if to underscore this point, Israeli air force planes overflew the Saudi military base at Tabuk.[66]

To counter the campaign to defeat the F-15 sale, the Saudis sent two younger, Western-educated princes to the United States to assist their ambassador in arguing the Saudi case: Bandar bin Sultan, son of the defense minister and an air force pilot, and Turki bin Faysal, son of the late King Faysal and the head of the Saudi security services. The U.S. ambassador to Saudi Arabia, John C. West, also campaigned hard for the sale.

What finally enabled the administration to defeat the move to disapprove the sale was a letter to Congress from Defense Secretary Harold Brown on May 9, 1978, stating built-in limitations in the proposed sale, including no capability for a data link to an early warning radar system, no long-range capability fuel pods, no bomb racks for ground attack capability, and only three—rather than five—hard spots to limit future conversion to a ground attack mission.[67] The Saudis also accepted the standard U.S. stipulation against transferring the F-15s to a third country without U.S. consent. This constraint was more an apparent than a real concession, since in any case no such transfers would be possible without provision of U.S.-controlled spare parts. The Saudis also implicitly indicated that they would not base the F-15s at Tabuk, their nearest base to Israel. (Such deployment would make little strategic sense since the aircraft were needed mainly to defend against potential threats in the south, the oil fields in the east, and the capital in central Arabia.) With these limitations assured, the Congress defeated a motion to deny the sale on May 15, 1978. As with the Peace Hawk program that provided U.S. support for the F-5s, a Peace Sum program was developed as an add on to support the F-15s.

For the Saudis, the psychological stakes involved in the F-15 sale had taken on at least as much importance as the military need. In Arab culture, a commitment once given and then taken away is an act of bad faith, and the F-15 sale had become for the Saudis a "litmus test" of U.S. friendship and of the U.S. commitment to the security of the Saudi regime and the Gulf generally. Thus, when the sale went through, the Saudis tended to overreact, seeing it as a major turning point in

U.S. Middle East policy toward more "evenhandedness" in dealing with its Arab friends. For them, it finally evened the score for the high political price the Saudis had paid in the Arab world and in OPEC for its friendship with the United States and its moderation on oil prices.

The United States also entertained somewhat unrealistic expectations of the significance of the F-15 sale. Far from seeing the sale as evening the score, the Americans expected a Saudi quid for the F-15 quo, particularly given the high political costs incurred in getting the sale through Congress. This lack of mutual understanding of the significance of the sale as perceived by the other party led to inevitable disillusionment and set the stage for the second "litmus test" in the military relationship, the AWACS sale.

In the meantime, Middle East security had begun to deteriorate. In January 1979, the shah of Iran went into exile, heralding the collapse of his regime and the rise of a militant Islamic republic under Ayatollah Rouhollah Khomeini. The Saudis were greatly shaken by the fall of the shah and also with the United States for appearing to do nothing to prevent it. As a result, the value of U.S. assurances of its commitment in support of the regime came into open question by Saudis.

At about the same time, perennial hostilities between North and South Yemen again flared up, causing concern in Riyadh and Washington. The United States agreed in late January to send a squadron of F-15s to Saudi Arabia, and an aircraft carrier group was deployed in the vicinity as a show of force. In March 1979, the United States sent two E-3A AWACS as well. It also agreed to accelerate arms transfers, including F-5 aircraft, to North Yemen, part of a package financed in large part by the Saudis.[68]

The third crisis in the region was the Soviet invasion of Afghanistan on December 27, 1979. The combination of the fall of the shah and the Soviet invasion of Afghanistan resulted in a full about-face in U.S. foreign policy priorities in the region, from preoccupation with political issues (the Camp David peace process) and social issues (human-rights violations) to preoccupation with security issues.[69]

In response to the increased security threat, the United States unilaterally began to examine steps for what became loosely referred to as the Persian Gulf Strategy. In his State of the Union address on January 23, 1980, President Carter stated that "an attempt by outside forces to gain control of the Persian Gulf region will be regarded as an assault on the vital interests of the United States, and such an assault will be repelled by any means necessary including military force."[70]

In order to carry out this policy, the United States undertook a number of steps. They included maintaining a permanent naval presence in the Indian Ocean and developing its capability to surge forces into the area by organizing a "rapid deployment force" (RDF) and by improving U.S. airlift forces to move the RDF more quickly. In addition, the United States sought access to air and naval facilities in Oman, Kenya, and Somalia and began to upgrade its facilities in Diego Garcia, in the mid-Indian Ocean.[71]

The United States maintained that it sought no bases, only access to facilities to support its peacetime presence, periodic exercises and deployments, and the ability to move forces into the area if necessary.[72] This position, however, was as much a recognition of political reality as of military need. In strictly military terms, Gulf and Indian Ocean security would have been far easier to accomplish with U.S. installations in the region (the closest, Diego Garcia, is several thousand miles away). Short of bases, access was the next best thing.

In addition, the United States sought cooperation with the Gulf states, particularly Saudi Arabia. This included building up local security capabilities and, if possible, prepositioning equipment to be ready for emergencies. In July 1979, the Carter administration announced its intention to seek congressional approval for a $1.2 billion sale for continuation of the Saudi National Guard modernization program. On December 12, Under Secretary of State Lucy Benson, in a statement to the House Foreign Affairs Committee, addressed the administration's decision to sell F-5 munitions to Saudi Arabia, including Sidewinder and Maverick missiles, laser-guided bombs, and cluster bombs. She said that the decision should be seen in the context of an "increasingly unstable" situation in the Gulf and that the State Department concurred with the Defense Department that the sale was militarily justifiable against a real threat.[73]

The Saudi reaction to the worsening security situation was characteristically ambivalent, made the more so by strains over Saudi refusal to endorse the Camp David process. Events had undermined Saudi faith not only in U.S. commitments to support the regime but also in the credibility of U.S. deterrence, particularly in the wake of the Soviet invasion of Afghanistan. Indeed, part of the justification for the subsequent AWACS sale was to restore both U.S. credibility as a reliable security partner and Saudi faith in U.S. commitment to regional security.[74]

In February 1980, National Security Council Advisor Zbigniew Brzezinski and Deputy Secretary of State Warren Christopher visited Riyadh to discuss the regional security situation with Crown Prince Fahd and to explore ways of enhancing closer military cooperation.[75] The Saudis wished for cooperation in the face of growing regional instability, but as a result of general Arab opposition to the Camp David process, they could not agree to any overt or direct cooperation with U.S. forces. For reasons of Arab politics and national pride, the Saudis preferred that

U.S. support be "over the horizon." In an effort to reassure themselves of the U.S. commitment, protect themselves in the face of a real threat, and avoid too close an entanglement with the United States, they responded to the Brzezinski-Christopher visit with a request for F-15 enhancements and E-3A AWACS aircraft.[76] This became the second "litmus test" of U.S. friendship.

In September 1980, the Iran-Iraq war broke out, making the Saudis more amenable to increased direct military cooperation with the United States and the United States more sympathetic to a favorable response to the Saudi arms request. By coincidence, the chairman of the U.S. Joint Chiefs of Staff, General David Jones, was visiting Saudi Arabia at the time. Together with Ambassador John West, he was able to respond immediately to a Saudi request for contingency assistance by offering to send E-3A AWACS aircraft to the Kingdom "within 24 hours." Ground radar, communications equipment, and about one hundred U.S. support personnel were also dispatched in order to fill gaps in Saudi air defenses in the vicinity of the oil fields.

The Saudis were particularly pleased with the rapid U.S. response, which received wide publicity.[77] Although some of the good will was dissipated by President Carter's statement (just before the 1980 presidential elections) that he would not agree to sell offensive enhancements such as bomb racks to Saudi Arabia, the lame duck Carter administration later decided that changed circumstances since 1978 (when the Brown letter to Congress ruled out enhancements) justified a favorable decision on the request. It communicated its views to the incoming Reagan administration, and on March 6, 1981, the new administration announced that it would soon notify Congress of its intention to sell missiles and fuel tanks to Saudi Arabia. On April 21, the White House announced its intention to sell an Air Defense Enhancement Package to the Saudis, which would also include five E-3A AWACS aircraft, AIM-9L air-to-air missiles, and KC-135 air-to-air tankers.[78]

The second litmus test was in many ways a repetition of the first, only far more intense. On the technical side, Secretary Brown's letter to Congress notwithstanding, the enhancement package was a natural outgrowth of Saudi air defense development programs beginning in 1963, and the specific arms requested were developed in large part out of U.S. studies of Saudi defense needs, the latest of which was Peace Hawk VII in 1981.[79] The sales made sense from the U.S. defense perspective also, by putting in place equipment compatible with U.S. equipment should the need for joint action arise. The deployment of a single squadron of F-15s to the Kingdom in 1979 demonstrated the logistical problems in trying to develop an "over-the-horizon" capability without some form of prepositioning of equipment, and placing it in the Saudi inventory was the next best thing.[80] The AWACS in particular was a case in point. The Saudis were determined to acquire an airborne radar system, and if they did not get the E-3A, the British had indicated that they would sell their equivalent, the Nimrod. Although partially compatible with U.S. communications, the Nimrod would be far less efficient than the E-3A in case the USAF was called in to help ward off an air strike on Saudi oil fields. Thus the AWACS sale made strategic sense to the United States as well as to Saudi Arabia.

The debate in Congress was in many ways a rerun of the 1978 F-15 debate except that the opponents had more time to prepare and, initially, came closer to success. The debate was also more intense. In a letter to the president in July 1980, sixty-eight senators went on record as opposed to the sale of AWACS and the F-15 enhancements package.[81] As with the F-15 sale, the air defense enhancements package was opposed mainly as a threat to Israel. Israeli Prime Minister Menachem Begin personally spoke out against the sale, and the American Israel Public Affairs Committee put out packets of materials opposing it. Opponents of the sale utilized the public and private testimony of every available critic of Saudi Arabia—including a noted but previously obscure historian from New Zealand named John B. Kelly, who added academic patina to their arguments.[82] The other side also mobilized. Saudi Arabia again sent Prince Bandar bin Sultan to help lobby for the sale, assisted by a Washington law firm. Former Carter administration officials, including former Secretary of Defense Brown, former Secretary of State Muskie, and the former ambassador to Saudi Arabia, John West, all spoke out in favor of the sale. On the academic side, Mazher Hameed of Georgetown University's Center for Strategic and International Affairs, R. D. McLaurin of Abbott Associates, and Lewis Snider at the Claremont Graduate School authored a study supporting the sale.[83]

In the end, however, it was the personal efforts of President Reagan, the White House staff, and the Republican leadership in the Senate that prevented congressional blocking of the sale. Since both houses had to disapprove to block the sale, the House—with a Democratic majority—was written off early, and administration efforts were concentrated on the Senate. With the administration focusing on domestic legislation through the summer, however, Senate opponents had seized the initiative and, by unofficial counts, thought they had as many as sixty-five votes by late August.[84] Nevertheless, on August 24, President Reagan formally proposed the sale to Congress.[85]

In the weeks that followed, lobbying became intense as President Reagan met personally with many senators to win them over. On October 14, the House, as expected, voted against the sale 301 to 111.[86] The following day, the Senate Foreign Relations Committee voted against the sale 9 to 8, but the vote was seen as an administration victory since the committee had earlier been opposed 14 to 3. Finally, on October 28, the effort to block the sale in the Senate was defeated by 52 votes.[87]

Working-Level Cooperation: After 1981

The Reagan administration's successful campaign for congressional support greatly reassured the Saudis of the U.S. commitment to regional security, and despite the debilitating effect of the intense and at times acrimonious congressional debate, the "litmus test" was passed. For the United States, the AWACS sale was far more than a litmus test. After only a month in office, the new administration announced that it was making security in the face of the Soviet threat its first priority in the Middle East rather than the Camp David peace process.[88] In developing this priority, the administration sought to create a "strategic consensus" among friendly regional states based on a balance of direct military aid and an over-the-horizon capability. The Saudi Air Defense Enhancement Package, therefore, was seen as an element of this new strategic consensus policy.

In fact, it was circumstances as much as political ideology that dictated U.S. Middle East priorities. The deteriorating security situation had already forced the Carter administration to develop its Persian Gulf strategy, which in retrospect did not appear all that different from the Reagan administration's strategic consensus policy. In the summer of 1982, the Israeli invasion of Lebanon began a process of refocusing U.S. Middle East policy concerns as well as regional attention back on the Arab-Israeli problem, placing U.S. policy toward the Gulf once again in the background. In February 1984, however, the Lebanese problem lost much of its urgency with the withdrawal of the U.S. Marines from Beirut, at least in the minds of U.S. policymakers.

All the while, plans proceeded apace for continued U.S. arms sales to Saudi Arabia. One item that was to take on political significance was the proposed sale of 400 basic Stinger air defense guided missile launchers, 400 missiles, and 300 additional missiles with associated training, support equipment, and spare parts at an estimated cost of $141 million. On February 29, 1984, the Reagan administration formally notified the Congress of the proposed sale under the terms of the Arms Export Control Act of 1976.[89] A similar sale was announced for Jordan. Both proposals were withdrawn in April, however, following a March 15 interview in the *New York Times* by King Hussein of Jordan together with resistance from Congress.

During the same period, the Iran-Iraq war, almost four years old, spread to the Gulf. In an effort to bring Iran to the bargaining table, Iraq began attacking oil tankers heading to and from Iran, using, inter alia, newly acquired French Exocet missiles. Iran began to retaliate; on May 13 and 14, Iranian aircraft attacked two Kuwaiti tankers, and on May 16, a Saudi tanker was hit inside Saudi territorial waters.[90]

The United States, which had tried to remain neutral in the Iran-Iraq war, became increasingly concerned over freedom of navigation in the Gulf. Several teams from the State and Defense departments visited the Gulf Cooperation Council states to discuss the threat. Finally, on May 21, President Reagan responded to the escalation of hostilities by sending a letter to King Fahd stating that the United States was prepared to use force if necessary to protect oil tankers in the Gulf.[91] On May 28, Reagan invoked Article 36(B)(1) of the Arms Export Control Act to transfer two hundred Stingers to Saudi Arabia without submitting the sale to the Congress, on the grounds that national security was being threatened by the situation in the Gulf.[92]

The United States found itself in a somewhat anomalous position. It was concerned not only for the security of Saudi Arabia but also for the security of the entire region. The United States, moreover, did not want to see either Iran or Iraq become either victor or vanquished. By March 1984, Washington had become concerned over the possibility of an Iranian breakthrough in the land war. By extending the war to the Gulf, Iraq hoped to restore the balance through threats to Iran's oil income and economic means to prosecute the war. Iraqi strategy, however, also threatened world oil supplies. Fortunately, due to the world oil glut, there was sufficient excess productive capacity worldwide to avoid a panic.

On the Saudi side, there was fear that the United States might not commit itself to the defense of the Kingdom, particularly in the wake of its withdrawal from Lebanon and the withdrawal of the Stinger sale proposal. President Reagan's willingness to use force if needed and the sale of two hundred Stingers was therefore highly reassuring in Riyadh. On the other hand, the Saudis were strongly opposed to U.S. or any foreign intervention in the Gulf unless absolutely necessary and were made somewhat nervous by the prospect implicit in the U.S. reassurance.

On June 5, 1984, two Saudi F-15s engaged two Iranian F-4s inside Saudi air space, shooting down at least one of them.[93] Both Americans and Saudis were by turns elated and anxious. The Americans were glad that the Saudis had shown themselves willing and able to defend themselves but were concerned over the possible further escalation of the Gulf war; the Saudis were elated that their air force was successful in defending Saudi air space but were also apprehensive about an escalation. The day before the engagement, King Fahd had told his cabinet, "Saudi Arabia is keen on pursuing quiet methods in dealing with the current situation in the Gulf with peaceful means and to avoid violence as much as possible. But, even so, we shall do all we can to defend our country and preserve our rights."[94] After the fact, the Saudi ambassador to Washington, Prince Bandar bin Sultan, added, "It is a pity it came to this, but we have to defend ourselves."[95]

To the relief of both Saudis and Americans, the incident did not result in a further escalation of hostilities and may have served as a deterrent. Thus, on balance, the events of the spring of 1984, despite the potential for increased ambivalence, reinforced the spirit of cooperation between the two countries. As in the past, the long tradition of cooperation continued to provide momentum in U.S.-Saudi military relations despite the vagaries of Middle East politics.

Notes

1. U.S. Department of State, *Foreign Relations of the United States,* vol. 4 (Washington, D.C.: Government Printing Office, 1943), p. 854 (hereafter cited as *FRUS* with volume and date).

2. Ibid.

3. *FRUS,* vol. 8, 1945, pp. 845 ff.

4. *FRUS,* vol. 6, 1949, pp. 1607–1611.

5. The Hashimite threat was discussed at the time of a meeting of the O'Keefe mission with the king. See ibid., p. 1613.

6. U.S. Department of State, *United States Treaties,* vol. 2, pt. 2, p. 1466 (hereafter cited as *UST* with volume number); U.S. Department of State, *Treaties and Other International Acts Series,* p. 2290 (hereafter cited as *TIAS* with page number).

7. *UST,* vol. 2, pt. 2, p. 1466; *TIAS,* p. 2289.

8. *TIAS,* p. 2812.

9. David Holden and Richard Johns, *The House of Saud* (London: Sidgwick and Jackson, 1981), p. 184.

10. Robert Lacey, *The Kingdom* (London: Hutchinson, 1981), p. 311.

11. Although the United States never formally joined the Baghdad Pact, or its successor, the Central Treaty Organization (CENTO), Washington considered the alliance to be a main element in containing Communist expansion into the Middle East. See Herman Finer, *Dulles over Suez: The Theory and Practice of His Diplomacy* (Chicago: Quadrangle Books, 1964), p. 18.

12. See "Memorandum for the Record" by the under secretary of state (Hoover), February 21, 1956 (Eisenhower Library [Abilene, Kansas], Dulles Papers, Israeli Relations, 1951–1957).

13. Robert H. Ferrell, ed., *The Eisenhower Diaries* (New York and London: W. W. Norton, 1981), p. 319.

14. For the text of the agreement, see *UST,* vol. 8, p. 403; and *TIAS,* p. 3790.

15. Dammam is the capital of the Eastern Province of Saudi Arabia and its principal city. Dhahran is, in fact, not a town at all, but consists of the airfield, the American Consulate General, the Aramco headquarters and compound, and—more recently—the University of Petroleum and Minerals.

16. Richard F. Nyrop, *Area Handbook for Saudi Arabia,* Foreign Area Studies (Washington, D.C.: American University Press, 1977), p. 212. Ambassador Eilts recalls the difficulty in obtaining congressional approval for completing the terminal. Personal communication, June 11, 1984.

17. The defections received wide press coverage at the time. See Holden and Johns, *The House of Saud,* p. 227.

18. *TIAS,* p. 2812.

19. U.S. Congress, Library of Congress, Congressional Research Service, Foreign Affairs and National Defense, "Saudi Arabia and the United States: The New Context in an Evolving Special Relationship" (Washington, D.C.: Government Printing Office, August 1981), p. 54.

20. Ibid. See also Anthony H. Cordesman, *The Gulf and the Search for Strategic Stability* (Boulder, Colo.: Westview Press; and London: Mansell Publishing; 1984), p. 204.

21. See U.S. Congress, Senate, *Multinational Corporations and United States Foreign Policy; Hearings Before the Subcommittee on Multinational Corporations of the Committee on Foreign Relations,* pt. 12, 94th Cong., 1st sess., 1975, and pt. 14, 2d sess., 1976 (Washington, D.C.: Government Printing Office, 1975 and 1976).

22. For a more detailed discussion of the Bunker mission, see Chapter 3.

23. See U.S. Congress, Senate, *Multinational Corporations,* pt. 12.

24. Ibid. Khashoggi also represented Raytheon and in 1970 became the agent of Northrop as well.

25. For an account of the British arms deal, see Anthony Sampson, *The Arms Bazaar: From Lebanon to Lockheed* (New York: Viking Press, 1977), pp. 174–181.

26. Ibid. See also U.S. Congress, House of Representatives, Committee on International Relations, Special Subcommittee on Investigations, *The Persian Gulf, 1975: The Continuing Debate on Arms Sales,* 94th Cong., 1st sess. (Washington, D.C.: Government Printing Office, 1976).

27. Sampson, *The Arms Bazaar,* pp. 158–164.

28. According to Holden and Johns, *The House of Saud* (p. 360), the original I-Hawk contract was set at $270 billion, but with extensive add ons the final contract, signed in 1977, was valued at $1 billion.

29. Sampson, *The Arms Bazaar,* p. 164.

30. Ibid., p. 163.

31. U.S. Congress, Senate, *Multinational Corporations,* pt. 12.

32. *New York Times,* June 1, 1973, p. 3.

33. U.S. Embassy, Jidda, "Corps of Engineers Activities in Saudi Arabia," briefing paper, 1973.

34. *UST,* vol. 16, p. 5830; *UST,* vol. 24, pt. 2, p. 7687.

35. U.S. Embassy, "Corps of Engineers."

36. Ibid.

37. *UST,* vol. 15, pt. 2, p. 5659; *UST,* vol. 18, pt. 3, p. 6413.

38. See U.S. Congress, Library of Congress, "Saudi Arabia and the United States."

39. U.S. Embassy, "Corps of Engineers."

40. Letter from Ambassador Eilts to Arabian Peninsula country director (William Brewer), Jidda, March 2, 1967, unclassified (Jidda Embassy files).

41. Holden and Johns, *The House of Saud,* p. 272.

42. The agreement was in the form of a Memorandum of Understanding signed by both countries on January 18, 1972. See Alvin J. Cottrell, ed., *The Persian Gulf: A General Survey* (Baltimore: Johns Hopkins University Press, 1980), p. 144.

43. Called upon to test-fire a machine gun, picked at random, Broady found himself surrounded by Abdallah and other National Guard notables on a makeshift desert range with carpets and gilded chairs for the VIP's. Attaché Broady did so well, including giving himself orders in Arabic, that Abdallah was overjoyed and fired the machine gun himself, in turn performing so well as to insure the success of the entire event.

44. "Memorandum of Understanding Concerning the Saudi Arabian National Guard Modernization Program." Signed at Jidda March 19, 1973. Entered into force March 19, 1975. Department of State *Bulletin,* May 27, 1973, p. 866.

45. Both the Aden regime and the leadership of the Dhufar rebellion, ultimately known as the Popular Front for the Liberation of Oman, were ideological descendants of the Arab Nationalists Movement, a radical group spawned in Beirut in the late 1940s. See David E. Long, *The Persian Gulf: An Introduction to Its Peoples, Politics, and Economics,* rev. ed. (Boulder, Colo.: Westview Press, 1978), pp. 55–56.

46. See U.S. Congress, Senate, Foreign Relations Committee, "U.S. Arms Sales Policy" (Washington, D.C.: Government Printing Office, 1977). By 1980, seven Peace Hawk studies had been completed.

47. With the F-15 order in 1978, Saudi purchases of F-5s were called back to a total of just over one hundred. See International Institute for Strategic Studies (IISS), *The Military Balance* (London: IISS, 1980-1981).

48. Holden and Johns, *The House of Saud,* p. 361.

49. For a comprehensive discussion of this Peace Hawk, see Cordesman, *The Gulf,* pp. 162–165.

50. Holden and Johns, *The House of Saud,* p. 361.

51. See Cordesman, *The Gulf.*

52. See "Testimony of James Akins, former Ambassador to Saudi Arabia," U.S. Congress, Senate, *Multinational Corporations,* pt. 14, pp. 419–420; Holden and Johns, *The House of Saud,* p. 354; and *Washington Post,* September 17, 1975.

53. See Cordesman, *The Gulf,* pp. 178–183; Holden and Johns, *The House of Saud,* p. 360; and *Los Angeles Times,* January 23, 1978.

54. For a discussion of Saudi army development in this period, see Cordesman, *The Gulf,* pp. 170–173.

55. Observations made to me by U.S. advisors at Khamis Mushayt in October 1980.

56. U.S. Arms Control and Disarmament Agency, *World Military Expenditures and Arms Transfers, 1966–1975 and 1969–1978* (Washington, D.C.: Government Printing Office, 1980), quoted in Cordesman, *The Gulf,* tables 6.1 and 6.2, pp. 201, 204.

57. Ibid.

58. See, for example, U.S. Congress, Senate, "U.S. Arms Sales Policy."

59. Ibid.

60. See U.S. Congress, Senate, *Multinational Corporations.*

61. Cottrell, *The Persian Gulf,* p. 146.

62. For a full account of the F-15 sale, see Cordesman, *The Gulf,* pp. 205–217.

63. Department of Defense spokesman, October 11, 1981, cited in ibid., p. 245, n. 22.

64. See, for example, American Israel Public Affairs Committee (AIPAC), *F-15s to Saudi Arabia: A Threat to Peace* (Washington, D.C.: AIPAC, January 1978).

65. Ibid.

66. See Henry Bradsher, "Israel Practiced Raids on Saudi Air Base," *Washington Star,* March 27, 1978. Actually, Israel had continuously violated Saudi air space since the 1967 Arab-Israeli war when the Israeli Defense Force occupied the Saudi islands of Tiran and Sanafir at the mouth of the Gulf of Aqaba.

67. Holden and Johns, *The House of Saud,* p. 487.

68. U.S. Congress, Library of Congress, "Saudi Arabia and the United States," p. 54.

69. For example, the area's strategic location and its significance to maintaining global strategic balance were listed first among U.S. interests in the region by Assistant Secretary of State Harold H. Saunders in "U.S. Relations with the Persian Gulf States," statement submitted to the House Foreign Affairs Committee on September 3, 1980. Department of State *Bulletin,* October 1980, p. 1.

70. Department of State *Bulletin,* February 1980, supplement B.

71. U.S. Congress, Library of Congress, "Saudi Arabia and the United States," pp. 57–59; and "U.S. Relations with the Persian Gulf States," p. 4. The RDF was renamed the U.S. Central Command (CENTCOM) on January 1, 1983.

72. "U.S. Relations with the Persian Gulf States," p. 4.

73. Department of State *Bulletin,* March 1980, pp. 63–64.

74. U.S. Department of State, "The Air Defense Enhancement Package for Saudi Arabia," August 1981, pp. 8–9.

75. U.S. Congress, Library of Congress, "Saudi Arabia and the United States," p. 59.

76. Ibid.

77. Ambassador West played host to a number of senior Saudi VIP's for rides on the aircraft.

78. U.S. Congress, Library of Congress, "Saudi Arabia and the United States," p. 64.

79. See Cordesman, *The Gulf,* pp. 278–280; and Scott Armstrong, "Saudi AWACS Just a Beginning of New Strategy," *Washington Post,* November 1, 1981.

80. See *Armed Forces Journal,* March 1979, p. 12.

81. U.S. Congress, Library of Congress, "Saudi Arabia and the United States," p. 61.

82. Kelly, a longtime antagonist of Saudi Arabia, was credited with writing the British case against Saudi Arabia in a territorial dispute involving the Buraymi Oasis in the 1950s. He published *Arabia, the Gulf and the West* (New York: Basic Books) in 1980 and in 1980-1981 was a fellow at the Woodrow Wilson Center for Scholars of the Smithsonian Institution. His views on Saudi Arabia were incisively set forth in the Spring 1981 issue of *International Security,* where he attempted to rebut "Security Considerations in the Persian Gulf," an article by Hermann Eilts (ambassador to Saudi Arabia, 1965–1970) in *International Security,* Fall 1980.

83. Mazher Hameed, R. D. McLaurin, and Lewis N. Snider, *An American Imperative: The Offense of Saudi Arabia* (Washington, D.C.: n.p., September 1981).

84. Personal interviews with Senate staff members.

85. *Washington Post,* August 25, 1981.

86. *Washington Post,* October 15, 1981.

87. *Washington Post,* October 29, 1981.

88. Cordesman, *The Gulf,* p. 278.

89. U.S. Department of State, "Press Guidance," March 2, 1984.

90. *Jordan Times,* May 19, 1984.

91. Wire service dispatches, May 22, 1984.

92. U.S. Department of State, "Press Guidance," May 29, 1984.

93. Saudi Press Agency, June 5, 1984.

94. Reuters, June 5, 1984.

95. Saudi Press Agency, June 7, 1984.

4
U.S.-Saudi Economic and Commercial Relations

From the very beginning, economic and commercial interests have been a major component of U.S.-Saudi relations. Few would have guessed, however, when the first U.S. oil concession was signed in 1933, that in fifty years Saudi Arabia would become the world's leading oil-exporting country, a major actor in the international financial system, and a major source of commercial opportunity for firms from the United States and from the rest of the world as well.

The development of economic and commercial relations falls roughly into two periods. The first, 1933 to 1973, was basically a period in which Saudi Arabia evolved from poverty to a major oil producer. By the 1960s, U.S.-Saudi economic and commercial relations had reached major proportions, but the full impact of their importance had not yet been totally appreciated by most U.S. policymakers. Bilateral economic and commercial relations grew apace but were almost always subordinated to political strategic concerns. Then, following the energy crisis of 1973-1974, Saudi Arabia seemed suddenly to emerge as a major economic power. In the succeeding years, U.S.-Saudi economic and commercial relations took on a priority all their own.

The Evolution of Commercial Relations: 1933–1973

Commercial relations between the United States and Saudi Arabia in the early years were conducted almost exclusively between the Saudi government and private U.S. firms, notably Aramco (Casoc). Such U.S. government involvement as occurred was usually limited to attempts to insure that U.S. firms were not unfairly discriminated against. When the United States did become more directly involved in commercial activities, the involvement was almost always justified on political or strategic grounds. The underlying rationale was that the political stability of the Kingdom depended in large measure on economic stability that in turn depended on the orderly development of its oil resources.[1]

This "benign neglect" on the part of the United States was not simply the result of the relative economic insignificance of Saudi Arabia in the early days. The United States, more than any other major trading country, had historically followed a policy of governmental noninterference in private business. One possible explanation for this is that most of the other major trading states had to export to survive. The United States, by contrast, blessed with abundant natural resources and a large domestic market, had never developed an export mentality to the same extent.

As a result of this minimalist foreign trade philosophy, U.S. corporations neither expected nor received the same kind of support from Washington that their major foreign competitors were able to obtain from their governments.[2] On the contrary, such practices were perceived in the U.S. public and private sector alike as conflicts of interest.

At the same time, U.S. public standards of overseas business ethics were also generally higher, perhaps also out of lack of a pressing need to export. It is inconceivable, for example, that any other major Western trading power would conduct public, highly publicized hearings on the alleged irregularities of its business firms abroad such as took place in the United States in the mid-1970s.[3]

That such a solid foundation for U.S.-Saudi commercial relations was developed by the early 1970s, therefore, had little to do with U.S. government policies. Rather, it was more the result of a number of perceptual factors that evolved during the years of Saudi personal business dealings with Americans. Saudis generally liked doing business with Americans, who had gained a reputation in the Kingdom as straightforward, reliable people who would deliver what they promised. This reputation was first gained by the oil men and later also by other Americans who came to the Kingdom to work.

Saudis also developed a respect for U.S. technology, which they came to regard as the best in the world. Since Saudis were loath to accept anything but the best, this became a tremendous competitive advantage, even on occasions when U.S. technology was not necessarily superior.

Another perceptual factor that aided in the establishment of close U.S.-Saudi commercial relations involved King Abd al-Aziz's original grant of the 1933 oil concession to Americans. The king was convinced that U.S. businessmen would not be used by the U.S. government to obtain a political toehold in the Kingdom in the manner of the European imperial powers.[4] This was one case in which Americans' concepts of conflicts of interest actually worked to their advantage. On the other hand, official U.S. noninvolvement in business affairs also became a cause of frustration to the Saudis. The U.S. government persistently demurred from promoting one U.S. firm over another in cases where the Saudis sought assistance in choosing the most qualified company for a contract.

Saudi business philosophy also enhanced the development of strong U.S.-Saudi commercial relations. Based on Islamic precepts, the Kingdom had one of the most laissez-faire business philosophies in the world. Moreover, the Hanbali school of Islamic jurisprudence to which Saudi Arabia subscribed, although the most conservative school in Sunni Islam on social and religious issues, was the most lenient and liberal on economic and commercial issues. It was therefore no accident that business dealings in the Kingdom were so wide open.[5] At the same time, a man's word was his bond, and great store was placed on interpersonal relations. It was perhaps fortunate that many early oil men came from Texas, where southern American notions of personal integrity in business dealings were also held in high regard.

At first, Aramco (Casoc) virtually monopolized U.S. commercial interests to the Kingdom. Following World War II, however, other U.S. firms began to appear, in conjunction either with Aramco construction and expansion or with U.S. military construction. For example, the engineering firm Bechtel arrived in the late 1940s to participate in the construction of the Tapline (the Trans-Arabian pipeline) from Saudi Arabia's Eastern Province to Lebanon for Aramco and also to construct Aramco's Ras Tanura refinery, the Jidda and Riyadh airports, and the Jidda pier. Another early arrival was Trans World Airlines (TWA), which obtained management and service contracts with Saudi Arabian Airlines at the time of its founding in 1945.[6]

In the 1960s, as the Saudis began to develop their nascent armed forces, U.S. defense contractors and suppliers joined the ranks of U.S. firms doing business in the Kingdom. Although Saudi defense spending in the 1960s now seems small in relation to expenditures in the 1970s and 1980s, it had nevertheless already reached hundreds of millions of dollars, and the strictly commercial aspects of U.S. military assistance were not lost on the U.S. government.[7] Characteristically, these considerations were generally seen by U.S. officials in the Kingdom as secondary to maintaining the quality and integrity of U.S. advice given to the Saudi military.[8]

Economic Relations: 1943–1973

U.S.-Saudi economic relations formally began with the extension of U.S. Lend-Lease aid to the Kingdom in 1943. The Lend-Lease agreement was undertaken in response to pleas for help from Casoc and was justified in terms of wartime national security.

With the outbreak of World War II, Saudi Arabia was on the brink of financial collapse. Its main source of revenue until that time had been receipts from the Hajj, or annual pilgrimage to Makkah. As a result of the war, the number of pilgrims had fallen to barely a trickle. Moreover, although Casoc had discovered oil, the war had brought the company's operations to a virtual standstill. Desperate to raise money, King Abd al-Aziz in January 1941 demanded a further advance from Casoc of $6 million for that year and hinted that he might need an additional $6 million per annum for the next five years. Another $4 million for 1941 was to be requested from the British.[9]

Casoc, which had already advanced the king a reported $6.8 million since 1939, was not anxious to set a precedent for underwriting the Saudi treasury.[10] On the other hand, it fully appreciated the Saudi position and thus reluctantly sought assistance from the U.S. government. In April 1941, James A. Moffett, chairman of the board of Caltex and Bapco (Bahrain Petroleum Company) and an old friend of the president, went straight to Roosevelt to request that the government loan Saudi Arabia $6 million a year for five years against oil products to be sold at a discount. Casoc also urged U.S. representations to the British to increase its subsidies to the Kingdom, but cautioned that it be made clear that such subsidies should not include British involvement in Casoc's concession.[11]

Roosevelt favored the plan, as did the State Department, but Navy Secretary Frank Knox advised the president on May 20 that Saudi oil was unsuitable for use by the U.S. Navy.[12] At that point, the State Department sought to extend aid to Abd al-Aziz through the newly enacted Lend-Lease program. It persuaded Casoc to have Abd al-Aziz formally request Lend-Lease aid, despite the risk of loss of face were the request to be turned down, and turned down it was.[13] Roosevelt, concerned over political repercussions from U.S. isolationists (the United States had not yet entered the war), preferred to turn to the British to bail out the king. The British, after all, had been the paramount political power in the region for over a century. Roosevelt did agree, however, that Lend-Lease to Britain could be used in part for Saudi Arabia.

By the beginning of 1943, U.S. attitudes had changed. One major difference was that the United States was by then fully engaged in the war, and its highest officials were finally becoming aware of the strategic importance of Saudi oil. Indeed, so successful were the efforts of Casoc and the State Department to educate the Roosevelt administration about the strategic value of the Casoc oil concession that the administration soon thereafter set out to buy it. As the State Department's economic advisor, Herbert Feis, put it, Casoc's owners "had gone fishing for a cod and had caught a whale."[14]

A second motivating factor leading to Lend-Lease for Saudi Arabia was the growing concern in Washington that the British intended to use their economic assistance to the Kingdom as a wedge to increase their political and oil interests, possibly at the expense of U.S. interests.[15] The immediate issue was a British plan to reform Saudi Arabia's chaotic currency by creating a central bank closely linked to London. Even the Anglophile U.S. (nonresident) minister to Saudi Arabia, Alexander Kirk, who favored the reform (with U.S. participation), warned lest the "increasingly discernible tendency toward British economic intrenchment in this area under war impact to a degree which might materially negate best intentioned post war agreements for equality of opportunity."[16]

With a sense of urgency absent two years earlier, President Roosevelt reacted favorably to a new recommendation by the State Department through the Lend-Lease administrator, Edward S. Stettinius, that Saudi Arabia be made eligible for Lend-Lease assistance. Even then it was more than a month before the decision was approved, a period characterized by intensive lobbying by the U.S. owners of Casoc. After being assured that the British had been consulted and had no objection, Roosevelt, on February 18, 1943, declared that the defense of Saudi Arabia was "vital" to the defense of the United States, and Saudi Arabia was thus eligible for Lend-Lease aid.[17] The United States actively joined Britain in insuring that Saudi Arabia would remain solvent, at least for the duration of the war.

Following the war, mounting oil revenues insured with finality that the Saudi government would no longer be forced into a hand-to-mouth existence, dependent upon foreign handouts for its economic survival. This did not mean, however, that its economic troubles were over. Although the Saudi Ministry of Finance was established in 1933, it continued to operate in the most rudimentary fashion according to the traditional personalized system of government extant in central Arabia for centuries. Monetary and fiscal affairs were in chaos.[18]

The United States was by now thoroughly awake to the budgetary and fiscal difficulties experienced by the Kingdom and to the importance of keeping Saudi Arabia solvent. In 1946, the Export-Import Bank loaned the Saudis $15 million and was to loan another $10 million in 1950.

The task of reforming the Kingdom's finances was far more formidable than probably even the British had imagined when they first pressed for reforms. One problem was that the political (and commercial) elites in Saudi Arabia seldom distinguished between public and private finance. God had blessed the country with oil wealth, and it was thus the rightful possession of any Saudi who could lay claim to it. Moreover, neither the aging King Abd al-Aziz nor his also aging finance minister, Abdallah

Sulayman, could fully grasp the growing complexities of government finance brought on by growing oil revenues. Islamic tradition, with its proscription of interest as usury, also contributed to the difficulties in instituting reform. Finally, traditionalist attitudes in the Kingdom had precluded the issuance of paper money. Legal tender was limited to Saudi silver riyals and British gold sovereigns. The fluctuating market in both precious metals further undermined monetary stability.

Partially in response to Saudi requests, and partly on its own initiative, the United States began offering technical assistance. In 1948, the Eddy-Mikesell mission (George Eddy, of the Office of International Finance of the Treasury Department, was a gold expert; Raymond F. Mikesell was from the State Department) was sent out to look at currency reform. In August 1950, John F. Greaney arrived in the Kingdom to help design an income tax (since abolished).[19] On January 17, 1951, a Point Four technical assistance agreement was signed. Although appropriate technical assistance projects were difficult to develop given Saudi Arabia's rudimentary governmental institutions, Point Four was to have a profound impact on Saudi finances.[20]

Under the auspices of the Point Four agreement, the United States in the summer of 1951 sent a financial mission under Arthur N. Young to reform the budgetary and administrative system of the Ministry of Finance and to improve the tariff system.[21] While modestly successful in these pursuits, the mission was far more successful in monetary reform. Prior to this time, most of the functions of a central bank had been undertaken by the Netherlands Trading Society (the "Dutch Bank"), which had been established in the 1920s to perform banking and other services for the Hajjis (Makkah pilgrims) from the Dutch East Indies (now Indonesia). Local banking was largely in the hands of traditional foreign-exchange dealers such as al-Ka'ki and Salim bin Mahfuz. On the recommendation of the Young mission, Saudi Arabia created the Saudi Arabian Monetary Agency (SAMA) to operate as the Kingdom's central bank. Its initial charter, promulgated on April 20, 1952, stated:

> 1. There is hereby created according to these regulations an institution to be called the Saudi Arabian Monetary Agency, the main operating office in which it shall start its functions to be in Jedda. It shall have branches and agencies in the places where required.
>
> 2. The objects of the Agency shall be:
>
> (a) To strengthen the currency of Saudi Arabia, to stabilize it in relation to foreign currencies, and to avoid the losses resulting to the Government and people from fluctuations in the exchange value of Saudi Arabian coins whose rates have not so far been fixed in relation to foreign currencies which form the major part of the Government's reserve;

(b) To aid the Ministry of Finance in centralizing the receipts and expenditures of the Government in accordance with authorized budget and in controlling payments so that all branches of the government shall abide by the government.[22]

In addition to these tasks, SAMA was also charged with regulating commercial banks and managing the Kingdom's reserves. SAMA opened its doors on October 4, 1952, and immediately embarked on a currency reform that included buying silver riyals at $.725 per ounce from a stabilization fund. The latter was created from dollars held by the Federal Reserve Bank of New York as collateral for silver the United States had transferred to Saudi Arabia under the Lend-Lease program, which was released for this purpose.[23]

Under its first governor, George Blowers (an American who had formerly been with the State Bank of Ethiopia), SAMA addressed the country's monetary problems with skill and imagination. One measure to stem riyal fluctuations was the issuance of Saudi gold sovereigns. The Saudis had previously ordered but had not circulated their own gold sovereigns. SAMA quickly began putting them into circulation at a ratio of forty riyals to one sovereign, making Saudi Arabia the only country in the world at that time with a fiduciary gold coin. (The sovereigns were withdrawn in 1954 after an influx of "counterfeit" gold sovereigns from abroad.)

Even more imaginative was the issuance of "Hajj receipts." In July 1953, SAMA inaugurated the issuance of scrip in denominations of 10, 100, and 1,000 Saudi riyals. Hajjis could obtain the scrip in exchange for their foreign currencies and redeem it at any local bank, thus facilitating currency transactions during the pilgrimage session. Because Hajj receipts were not considered legal tender, their acceptance was not resisted by the general public as the issuance of paper currency would have been; and at any rate the Hajj receipts were fully backed by gold and silver. By August 7, 1953, SR23 million worth of Hajj receipts had been issued; by September 10, only 30 percent of that had been redeemed.[24] By 1955, when a rise in the world price of silver caused Saudi riyals to be smuggled out of the country, "Hajj receipts" had become accepted as currency throughout the country.

When King Saud succeeded his father in 1953, U.S.-Saudi economic relations began to suffer along with political relations. In 1954, the Kingdom revoked the Point Four agreement, and all Point Four personnel were ordered to leave the country on the grounds that the $1.7 million allocation was too small in comparison with the sums given Israel.[25] When Faysal replaced his brother as prime minister in 1962 and as king in 1964, economic relations improved, but by and large the Saudis had begun to acquire economic technical assistance from the marketplace. For example, the country's first five-year development plan, drawn up by the Central Planning Office (later the Ministry of Planning) and approved in September 1970, was drafted in large measure with the technical assistance of the Stanford Research Institute of California.[26]

U.S. government technical assistance to Saudi Arabia during the 1960s was mainly focused in the military field (see Chapter 3) and in minerals exploration. In 1963, the United States Geological Survey (USGS) and Aramco, under joint U.S.-Saudi sponsorship, published a geological map of the country. In August 1963, an agreement was signed providing for USGS to conduct further mineral explorations.[27] During the 1960s, the head of the USGS mission was Dr. Glenn Brown, who had first gone to Saudi Arabia in the 1940s and could fairly be called the "grand old man of Arabian geology."

Despite the ups and downs in Middle East politics in the 1950s and 1960s, U.S.-Saudi economic and commercial relations remained close. On the fiscal side, the United States by the late 1960s was already urging SAMA to place more of its foreign-exchange holdings in longer-term U.S. government securities, a harbinger of things to come in the 1970s. The Saudi's need for Western technology and technical assistance, their preference for U.S. technology and business practices, and the U.S. commercial, political, and strategic interests in Saudi oil and in the growing purchasing power of the Kingdom all contributed to insulate economic relations to a great degree from the divisive Middle Eastern political issues of the day.

Economic and Commercial Relations in the Post–Energy Crisis World: 1973–1984

In the years immediately preceding the world energy crisis of 1973-1974, there was a growing realization in the United States of Saudi Arabia's expanding importance in world trade and economic affairs. In June 1973, just prior to the energy crisis, Assistant Secretary of State Joseph J. Sisco, in enunciating U.S. policy objectives in the Arabian Peninsula–Gulf region to the House Foreign Affairs Committee, included "enhancing of our commercial and financial interests."[28] He listed it last, however, concentrating instead on supporting regional collective security (the Two Pillar Policy) and focusing on Iranian-Saudi cooperation.

Just fourteen months later, on August 7, 1974, the new assistant secretary, Alfred L. Atherton, speaking to the same group, stated:

> Most of the Gulf states have suddenly become financial powers. In many cases, their economies are no longer able to absorb the enormous increase in oil revenues. Their growing financial power and control of energy resources give them a potential influence in world affairs far in excess of their population or military strength.[29]

While still defending the Two Pillar Policy, Atherton added,

> There is now, however, an additional objective in light of the vast increase in oil revenues, and that is to assist and encourage the countries of the region to recycle their revenues into the world economy in an orderly and nondisruptive manner.[30]

Behind this new focus were considerable fears expressed around the world that the world financial system would not be able to recycle the huge amounts of petrodollars being amassed by Saudi Arabia and other oil producers, resulting in a massive, worldwide liquidity crisis. Moreover, it was also feared in some quarters that petrodollars would be used by Arab producers to disrupt world money markets for political purposes. In the United States in particular, there were fears that Arab petrodollars would be used to buy U.S. firms, control segments of the U.S. economy, and possibly to inhibit Jewish financial interests.[31]

The combination of challenge, opportunity, and anxieties created by the massive accumulation of foreign-exchange holdings by Saudi Arabia and other OPEC oil producers following the energy crisis resulted in a high level of ambivalence in U.S. economic relations with Saudi Arabia reminiscent of other areas of the relationship.[32] On the one hand, the United States welcomed investment of petrodollars. This policy was actually one of long standing with regard to all foreign investment and was in keeping with the U.S. open door economic philosophy. Moreover, it was adopted not to accommodate foreign investors or governments but because it provided substantial advantages to the United States. Petrodollar investments in particular were seen to work to U.S. benefit "by giving OPEC nations a stake in our economic well being, providing needed investment capital for the United States, and providing additonal strengths in our relations with the oil producing nations."[33]

Accordingly, the United States set out to facilitate Saudi and other OPEC investment. It did so primarily in two ways. One was an understanding reached in early 1974 to treat the Saudis' investments in the United States confidentially, an issue of extreme sensitivity to them.[34] The second was an arrangement between the U.S. Treasury Department and SAMA, worked out in late 1974, for SAMA purchases of U.S. government securities through the Federal Reserve Bank of New York.

The New York Federal would notify SAMA of Department of Treasury public offerings of securities with maturity of more than one year and of the terms and conditions of the sale. If SAMA indicated a desire to purchase part of the public offering, the New York Federal would place a noncompetitive tender on behalf of SAMA and notify SAMA of the average price and amount due on the settlement date.[35]

At the same time, on the other hand, there was concern in the U.S. government over the adequacy of its system for monitoring growing OPEC and other foreign investment in the United States. In 1974, the Treasury Department began a major four-year overhaul of its Treasury International Capital (TIC) Reporting System, which, in conjunction with the Securities and Exchange Commission, keeps track of foreign portfolio investment. Reporting was further upgraded by the Domestic and Foreign Investment Improved Discharge Act of 1977 (Title II of P.L. 95-213).[36]

On May 6, 1975, Executive Order 11858 created the Committee of Foreign Investment in the United States (CFIUS), chaired by the Treasury Department and including representatives of the Departments of State, Defense, and Commerce; the Office of the U.S. Trade Representative; and the Council of Economic Advisors. Its mission was to monitor the impact of foreign direct and portfolio investment and to review investments that had major implications for U.S. national interests.[37] The executive order also called for the creation of the Office of Foreign Investment in the United States (OFIUS) within the Department of Commerce to provide analytical support, data, and recommendations to the committee.[38]

In 1976, the International Investment Survey Act was passed (22 U.S.C. 3101), further upgrading the acquisition and analysis of information on foreign direct and portfolio investment. Information on foreign ownership and purchases of U.S. farmland was added in the Agricultural Foreign Investment Disclosure Act of October 14, 1978 (P.L. 95-460).

Ambivalence in U.S. economic relations with Saudi Arabia was particularly pronounced among those who were concerned that OPEC, and its Arab members in particular, were acquiring "a 'money weapon' to accompany their near monopoly control over the supply of oil."[39] As an Arab state and OPEC's key producer, Saudi Arabia came under particular scrutiny. In 1975 and 1976, the Subcommittee on Multinational Corporations of the Senate Foreign Relations Committee, chaired by Senator Frank Church of Idaho, held extensive hearings on corrupt practices overseas in which considerable attention was paid to business operations in the Kingdom.[40] In 1978, Congressman James H. Schever, chairman of the Subcommittee on Domestic and International Scientific Planning Analysis and Cooperation of the House Committee on Science and Technology, scheduled hearings on technology transfer to OPEC countries.[41]

The most persistent congressman in investigating possible threats to U.S. economic interests from Saudi Arabia and other Arab oil-producing states, however, was Benjamin S. Rosenthal, a Democrat from New York. From the mid-1970s until his death in early 1983, Rosenthal scheduled multiple hearings on OPEC investments in the United States, concentrating to a great degree on Saudi Arabia.[42] Rosenthal was particularly concerned about the possibility of OPEC countries' adopting investment policies injurious to the United States, not so much on economic grounds but on "emotion or hysteria or politics."[43] He was also concerned over the possibility of Arab oil producers' buying controlling interest in or exerting undue pressure (through contractual relationships) on firms in the defense industry or other strategically sensitive sectors of the U.S. economy.[44] Despite government witnesses' assurances that no such scenarios appeared likely, Rosenthal stated that he had no doubts whatsoever thay they did[45] and called on numerous witnesses who supported his view.[46]

The Treasury Department's position was summed up when the assistant secretary of treasury for international affairs, C. Fred Bergsten, appeared before Rosenthal's subcommittee in 1979. He testified:

- that OPEC investments in the United States, although large in absolute terms, represented a small share of every category of foreign investment in the United States and an extremely small share of total investments, domestic and foreign, in this country;
- that the interests of the OPEC investors themselves, and their clearly stated policies, suggested little likelihood that they would ever try to disrupt our economy or financial system by withdrawing their investments here;
- that, if they did, we had ample defenses against actual disruption through the workings of the private banking system, existing legislation, and cooperation from other major countries;
- that it would not be in the interest of the United States to deter OPEC investments in this country any more than it would be to deter investments from other countries, and hence we respected the desire of some OPEC countries to maintain confidential treatment of their investments here, as clearly authorized by law; and
- that a reversal of these policies, by changes in the law or in current practice, would clearly discourage foreign investment for no apparent public purpose.[47]

The last two points were of particular importance, dealing with confidentiality and the traditional U.S. policy of welcoming foreign investment on a nondiscriminatory basis. The confidentiality issue actually became involved in the broader constitutional issue of separation of powers between executive privilege and the congressional investigatory responsibility. Senator Church, Congressman Schever, and Congressman Rosenthal had all requested detailed information on the amounts and nature of Saudi and other OPEC investments in the United States.[48] Requests had been directed to the Treasury Department, the Federal Reserve Bank, the Central Intelligence Agency, and the State Department. Following the Treasury Department's lead, all the agencies turned down the request.[49]

The Treasury Department took the position, adopted by the executive branch, that it was legally barred from disclosing confidential information on Saudi and other foreign investments according to the Bretton Woods Agreements Act (22 U.S.C. 286 et seq.). The act provides for safeguarding confidentiality.[50] In 1978, Congressman Schever contested this view and requested Richard Ehlke, a legislative attorney with the Congressional Research Service, to prepare a legal report to that effect.[51] Following Rosenthal's failure to acquire information a year later, he asked the General Accounting Office (GAO) for an opinion. In its reply, the GAO General Counsel upheld the view that the Treasury Department did not violate the law by maintaining confidentiality. The report added, however, that confidentiality did not "affect Congress' access," but, rather, was "designed to restrict public disclosure."[52] To many a government bureaucrat seeking to guard confidentiality, that was tantamount to the same thing; but in any event, the constitutional issue remained moot.

Confidentiality was important to U.S.-Saudi economic and commercial relations because of the Saudis' extreme sensitivities. Efforts to limit or restrict foreign investments in the United States, however, were a much broader and more fundamental issue. By March 1975, nearly forty bills had been introduced in the Congress, ostensibly to monitor foreign investment along lines mentioned above, but in many cases designed specifically to halt Arab investment in the United States for fear of adverse political effects to Israel of closer U.S.-Arab financial ties. The U.S. banking community, however, realizing the folly of reversing the historical U.S. policy of free capital movement, opposed such actions. In fact, much of the subsequent effort given to combating the Arab boycott of Israel, according to a prominent Jewish financial expert, was to force attention away from attempts to limit foreign investment.[53]

U.S. commercial policy toward Saudi Arabia and other Arab oil-producing states following the energy crisis was no less ambivalent. It was quickly seen that, in order to offset the balance-of-payments deficit of growing oil imports as well as to recycle petrodollars, the United States would have to promote exports to the oil-producing countries. Moreover, export promotion was good for the country in terms of the jobs it created. Of course, the United States' major trading partners also saw the advantages of the growing Middle East market, and competition was fierce. Thus, in 1974, the Commerce Department created a new office, the Commerce Action Group on the Near East (CAGNE), to assist businesspeople and to promote U.S. trade expansion in the region. In the field, the American Embassy in Jidda and the Consulate General in Dhahran were also extremely supportive of U.S. business in the Kingdom, developing a rapport rare in most countries overseas.

At the same time, however, the Congress began passing or strengthening laws that had the opposite effect, that of impeding trade to the Middle East. The laws that had the most adverse effect on trade in the 1970s were the antiboycott amendments, U.S. tax disincentives, and the Foreign Corrupt Practices Act.

U.S. Antiboycott Amendments

The Arab boycott of Israel has been in existence since soon after the creation of the Israeli state. For years, few people in the United States paid much attention to the boycott, but in the 1960s, as Arab oil wealth and attendant economic and political influence increased, U.S. supporters of Israel began to be concerned over the implications for U.S.-Israeli relations. In 1965, this concern was registered in amendments to the Export Control Act of 1949 (P.L. 89-63, 79 Stat. 209 [1965]), which were also included in the Export Administration Act of 1969 (50 U.S.C. 2401 et seq.).

These early amendments were mainly symbolic, and their significance was primarily that they established a precedent for U.S. opposition to the Arab boycott. They embodied a general declaration of policy against boycotts of friendly countries and required U.S. firms to report to the Commerce Department all instances in which they had been requested to participate in such boycotts. The 1969 act also permitted the government to deny export licenses in order to implement antiboycott policy, but there is no record that this provision was ever activated.

The Arab boycott became a far greater issue following the Arab oil embargo of 1973-1974, stemming from general U.S. resentment over gas shortages, higher prices, and a perceived linkage between U.S. dependence on oil and the strength of U.S.-Israeli relations. In 1975-1976, twenty-two antiboycott amendments were introduced in the Congress and a number of others in state legislatures.[54]

The Ford administration attempted to moderate the antiboycott drive to avoid jeopardizing U.S.-Arab relations and U.S. exports. It did, however, strengthen the Commerce Department's reporting requirements and prohibited compliance with any boycott requirements discriminating on the basis of race, color, or creed. In 1976, the Justice Department brought suit against the Bechtel Corporation for violating Section 1 of the Sherman Antitrust Act of 1890 prohibiting "every contract, combination, . . . or conspiracy in the restraint of trade or commerce among the several states or with foreign nations." Bechtel was accused of complying with Saudi requirements prohibiting contracting firms from dealing with blacklisted firms in the fulfillment of their contract (that is, the use of blacklisted subcontractors). The case was negotiated out of court on January 10, 1977,[55] and although the outcome is binding only on Bechtel, it did lay down some general guidelines:

- prohibiting a U.S. company under contract in an Arab country from refusing to deal with blacklisted firms in the fulfillment of the contract;
- prohibiting such a company from requiring that other parties refuse to deal with blacklisted firms; or
- prohibiting discrimination against blacklisted firms by any U.S. firm helping an Arab government or firm solicit, evaluate, or select bids.[56]

Two acts passed by the Congress during this period, together with the Sherman Antitrust Act, make up the bulk of U.S. antiboycott legislation. They are the Tax Reform Act of 1976 (P.L. 94-455) and the Export Administration Act Amendments of 1977. The Tax Reform Act provisions, implemented by the Treasury Department, deny offenders of antiboycott legislation their right to foreign tax credits, tax benefits to "domestic international sales corporations" (DISCs), and deferral of taxation of foreign income derived from business in countries requiring participation in a boycott.[57] The Export Administration Act Amendments of 1977 were passed with the strong endorsement of newly elected president Carter, who had promised in his campaign to seek stiffer antiboycott legislation. The 1977 amendments, implemented by the Commerce Department, were subsequently incorporated into the Export Administration Act of 1979 (P.L. 96-72). The act and implementing Export Administration Regulations[58] set out the guidelines for U.S. firms doing business in boycotting countries. Violation carries a maximum fine of not more than five times the value of the exports involved or fifty thousand dollars, whichever is greater, or imprisonment of not more than five years, or both. A civil fine may be imposed up to ten thousand dollars per violation.[59]

Antiboycott legislation has been controversial since its inception. No one questioned the sovereign right of any country to boycott goods and services of another country, an action referred to as a primary boycott. The United States, however, has made a legal distinction between primary boycotts and secondary and tertiary boycotts. A secondary boycott involves blacklisting third-country firms that in their business have close dealings with the boycotted country. A tertiary boycott involves prohibiting components or services of blacklisted firms from being used by nonblacklisted third-country firms in fulfilling contractual obligations in the boycotting country. The intent of the U.S. legislation was to oppose the latter two categories.

Even then, however, the United States was not historically on the firmest legal ground in that it has itself engaged in secondary and tertiary boycotts, such as provisions in the Trading with the Enemy Act and the Mutual Defense Assistance Control (Battle) Act. Indeed, the State Department originally opposed the 1965 antiboycott amendments on grounds that it would make implementation of U.S. boycotts all the harder.[60] According to a former State Department deputy legal advisor, the United States is the "Olympic Champion" of political trade controls.[61]

A second area of controversy and misperception involved racial and religious discrimination, which has been used to justify antiboycott legislation. Saudi Arabia, in particular, had been singled out for requiring that religious preference be stated on visa applications. The Arab boycott, however, as interpreted by Saudi Arabia and all Arab states, is political in nature (as is U.S. antiboycott legislation).

Despite these differences of opinion, the antiboycott legislation has not been an insurmountable obstacle to those U.S. firms wishing to do business with Saudi Arabia and other Arab states. From businesspeople's point of view, the most onerous aspect has been that which deals with responses to boycott-related queries. For example, it is illegal to respond to queries for information that is already public, such as stockholders' reports. On the other hand, the 1977 amendments, much of the substance of which was negotiated by the Business Roundtable in consultation with pro-Israeli interest groups, did take into account business concerns, particularly in delineating what type of behavior in boycotting countries is permissible and what is not.[62] This delineation also helped Saudi Arabia, which was cooperative in accommodating Americans, to meet antiboycott regulations, providing such accommodation did not compromise its own adherence to the Arab boycott. In sum, the antiboycott legislation has provided an avenue for making a political statement in support of Israel that, while it has been an irritant to U.S. firms doing business in Saudi Arabia and the Arab world, has not by itself constituted an insurmountable burden to U.S. commercial interest in the region.

U.S. Tax Disincentives

In the 1970s and early 1980s, taxes on personal income earned abroad had become the most powerful disincentive to U.S. exports to Saudi Arabia.[63] No other major trading state has had such stringent tax liabilities for overseas earned income.

Up to the 1950s, there were very few U.S. tax liabilities for citizens working overseas, in recognition of the linkage between enhanced exports and Americans living abroad. In the 1950s, the U.S. Tax Code was amended to place a twenty-thousand-dollar ceiling on exemption of overseas income. In those days, that was a significant amount of money, but by the 1970s it had shrunk considerably due to inflation. Nevertheless, in 1976, the ceiling was lowered to fifteen thousand dollars, and because of changes in the method by which it was computed, it could in practice be as little as three thousand dollars. Moreover, many former employee allowances were discontinued, and a 1976 U.S. Tax Court ruling held that for computing the exemption, allowances such as those for housing had to be computed at their full overseas value rather than at the equivalent value in the United States. This meant that in Saudi Arabia, where a modest three- or four-bedroom house could rent for as high as fifty thousand dollars per year, housing and cost-of-living allowances had to be considered earned income. Thus, tax bills for many Americans could exceed their cash income.[64]

Finally, after realizing the damage to the balance of payments that this situation was causing in lost exports to the Arab states in particular, the Congress passed the Foreign Earned Income Act of 1978 (26 U.S.C. 911 and 913) to give some relief. Among the most successful "lobbyists" were members of the American Businessmen's Association in Riyadh. They lobbied every member of Congress who passed through, including Senator Jacob Javits of New York, who appeared impressed by their contention that the tax provisions were responsible for the drop in the proportion of U.S. employees in U.S. firms in Saudi Arabia from 65 percent in 1976 to 35 percent in 1980.[65]

The 1978 act, however, was too narrowly construed, and the Internal Revenue Service (IRS) regulations were so complex that they did little to alleviate the problem. Indeed, the IRS felt constrained to assign a full-time employee to the American Embassy in Jidda just to try to explain the regulations to private Americans working in the Kingdom.[66] Finally, in 1981, relief was obtained in the Economic Recovery Act of 1982,[67] which increased exempted income and excluded from the computation many of the allowances. Beginning in 1982, exempted income was set at $70,000, to increase $5,000 each year to 1985, when it would be $90,000.

The Foreign Corrupt Practices Act of 1977

Congressional investigations into the activities of multinational corporations, revealing illegal payments in Saudi Arabia and other countries, culminated in the passage of the Foreign Corrupt Practices Act of 1977 (P.L. 95-213, Title I, 91 Stat. 1494). The act required new accounting procedures intended to prevent the concealment of illegal payments to foreigners, whether agents or officials. It also prohibited bribery of those foreign officials who exercised any discretionary authority over government contracting decisions with private firms. The maximum fine for violating the antibribery provisions was one million dollars for a corporation and ten thousand dollars and/or five years imprisonment for an individual.

The U.S. firms most affected, including those doing business in Saudi Arabia, were highly critical of the act, not because of any desire to perpetuate corrupt practices, but because the act was considered to be so vaguely written and poorly drafted that it added a significant burden on the companies to determine what was and was not permissible. A strong lobbying effort was mounted to have it repealed.[68]

The Saudis did not entirely share that opposition to the act. "If campaigning for bribery [i.e., against the Foreign Corrupt Practices Act] makes no sense to Americans," commented a former Saudi commercial attaché to the United States, "it makes no sense to Saudis either."[69] Indeed, the Saudis, during the 1970s, were enacting their own anticorruption regulations. Differences between U.S. and Saudi regulations were primarily a reflection of different cultures and ethical codes. For example, it is an almost implicit assumption in the U.S. law that the payment of commissions to foreign agents is a principal vehicle for evading the law. By contrast, use of agents is an accepted way of conducting business in Saudi Arabia. Nevertheless, Saudi regulations limit agent commissions to 5 percent of the value of the contract and require the relationship between agent and client to be put in writing.

In the main, the Saudis welcomed close commercial relations with the United States. With the quantum increase in oil revenues after 1973, Saudi development spending increased in geometric proportions. Government expenditures increased from $2.6 billion in 1973 to $43.1 billion by 1979.[70] Whereas the First Five Year Plan (1970–1975) had an initial budget of $9.2 billion, the Second Five Year Plan (1975–1980) projected expenditures of $141 billion.[71] Thus, commercial opportunities in the Kingdom burgeoned. U.S. firms continued to hold roughly 20 to 23 percent of the Saudi import market, and hence reaped substantial revenues that helped the U.S. balance of payments in a period of growing U.S. oil imports. The fact that they were not able to increase their market share was, in the Saudi view, primarily the fault of the U.S. government. The Saudis viewed the antiboycott and tax legislation already mentioned as examples of the United States' "shooting itself in the foot." Many Saudis expressed the view that they, through their efforts to accommodate U.S. exporters, were promoting U.S. trade to the Kingdom more than was the U.S. government.

Among Saudi businessmen and government officials, a major area of concern in overall economic and commercial relations was the persistence of pejorative stereotypes with which Saudis were characterized in the United States. They found the images of corrupt business agents and greedy "oil shaykhs" offensive. "You may be sure," wrote one Saudi, "that the selection by an agency of the U.S. government of an 'Arab Sheikh' with lots of money trying to buy American Congressmen did not make Saudi Arabians think better of the United States. Beyond bad taste and insensitivity this Abscam operation . . . tells us about the need for change in the American attitude toward Arabs. . . ."[72]

The Saudis were more ambivalent about U.S.-Saudi economic relations. With their mounting trade surplus and foreign-exchange holdings, they welcomed U.S. efforts to accommodate greater investments in the United States. They were well aware that with limited investment opportunities at home, they had little alternative except to place the bulk of their holdings in the financial markets of the West, particularly the United States. On the other hand, they realized that by placing large investments in the United States, they would be vulnerable to restrictions or even seizure of their assets for political reasons.[73] The Saudis also worried that large surpluses placed in long-term foreign investments would shrink due to inflation and currency devaluations, and they were generally convinced that oil was a better long-term investment if left in the ground.[74] In addition, they found themselves under pressure from the United States and other Western governments as well as from international financial organizations, such as the World Bank and the International Monetary Fund, to divert some of their holdings to foreign aid. Although they fully intended to become one of the world's leading foreign-aid donors (and indeed did so), they did not wish to be placed in the position of being pressured to meet every world financial need.[75]

Development of a Special Relationship: The U.S.-Saudi Joint Commission

Fears of Saudi Arabia's developing a "money weapon" were ill founded. Far from being the financial buccaneers they were portrayed to be, the Saudis pursued foreign investment policies that were, if anything, too conservative. One could find more hysteria in the New York Stock Exchange than in SAMA. Liquidity and security were the Saudis' main priorities, even to the extent of paying negative interest rates in Swiss and West German banks.[76] Moreover, although they obtained a seat on the International Monetary Fund (IMF) in 1978, the Saudis evinced little desire to play an active role in the management of the international financial system.

The Saudis did see a political connection to their petrodollar holdings, however, though not as a money weapon. On the contrary, they sought to use their new economic status to increase cooperation, not confrontation, with the United States. In substance, this policy was nothing new. Since the famous meeting between President Roosevelt and King Abd al-Aziz aboard the USS *Quincy* in 1945, the Kingdom had sought reassurances from the United States of its commitment to the well-being of Saudi Arabia and other friendly Arab states.

Two new aspects arose, however. One was the Saudi desire to ease the strains in U.S.-Saudi relations created by the October 1973 Arab-Israeli war and subsequent oil embargo. In discussing the strengthening of economic ties with the United States in early June 1974, Prince Fahd noted the benefits of enhanced U.S.-Saudi economic cooperation to Saudi economic development, but added, "what is most important is a commitment that America's relationship with Saudi Arabia is an integral part of its relationship and attitude toward the Arab world's problems. . . ."[77]

The other new aspect was the Saudi's determination that, with their new oil and financial power, Saudi economic relations with the United States, and indeed with the major industrial countries of the West generally, be placed on more equal terms. In short, what they sought was a "special relationship."

This desire fell on very sympathetic ears in Washington. The new concept of a U.S.-Saudi "special relationship" was coined by John Sawhill, then head of the Federal Energy Administration, in hearings before the Senate Subcommittee on Multinational Corporations.[78] In the economic area, the advantages were obvious. The stated U.S. aim of recycling petrodollars could better be served, commercial opportunities for U.S. business could be enhanced, and expanded Saudi reliance on U.S. technical assistance in economic development could encourage closer cooperation on broader political issues of mutual interest. Beyond that, however, there seems to have been a recognition that, in the wake of the energy crisis, a permanent alteration to the world economic system had taken place.[79] Walter H. Donaldson, then under secretary of state for security affairs, expressed this view in March 1974: "It is evident that the international environment has dramatically changed

. . . [and that] we must recognize that interdependence is a fact, not a choice."[80]

From this mutual interest in economic cooperation the U.S.-Saudi Joint Commission was born. Prince Fahd was the driving force on the Saudi side and Secretary of Treasury William Simon and Secretary of State Kissinger guided the U.S. side.

Joint economic commissions were not, in fact, a new idea. In 1958, a Joint U.S.-Canadian Committee on Trade and Economic Affairs was established and met up to 1970. In 1961, a Japan-U.S. Economic Conference was created, under which for a number of years the secretaries of state, treasury, commerce, and labor met with their counterparts alternately in Japan and the United States. With this historical precedent, the idea of creating a joint commission to further economic cooperation with Saudi Arabia first came to light in a proposal from the American Embassy in Jidda in January 1974. The embassy argued that such a high-level forum would bring the two countries closer together politically, in the wake of the October war; would assist the Saudis to apply their oil wealth more effectively to economic development (which would also induce them to continue to produce oil at a high level); and would also help to expand U.S. exports for capital goods and technological services at a time when it appeared that higher oil prices would produce huge balance-of-payments deficits.[81]

From this beginning, the Americans and Saudis began discussions that resulted in a joint U.S.-Saudi statement of agreement to expand economic cooperation and to negotiate a U.S. supply of weapons for Saudi defense requirements.[82] Then, during a visit of Prince Fahd to Washington, he and Secretary of State Kissinger on June 8, 1974, issued a joint statement on Saudi Arabian–U.S. cooperation. The statement called for a joint commission on economic cooperation to be headed by the U.S. secretary of the treasury and the Saudi minister of finance and national economy. It also called for a second joint commission "to review programs already underway for modernizing the Kingdom's defense requirement, especially as they relate to training."[83]

The April and June statements led many outside observers to assume that the joint commissions were simply a quid pro quo for lifting the oil embargo.[84] Some went farther and speculated that it was an attempt by the United States to obtain secure oil supplies from Saudi Arabia bilaterally despite the stated U.S. policy calling for a multilateral approach.[85] As the previous discussion indicates, such was not the case. Moreover, within five months the United States created five other joint commissions in the Middle East (with Iran, Israel, Egypt, Jordan, and Tunisia) and one with India.

At the outset, the Americans and the Saudis had slightly differing perceptions of what the joint commissions signified. For the Saudis, a visible sign of U.S. commitment to the Kingdom was very important, as indicated by the inclusion of a joint commission on military affairs. As it turned out, that commission was stillborn, its substantive mission already being adequately performed by USMTM, the Corps of Engineers, and other programs. The Saudis also saw in the Joint Commission for Economic Cooperation (called henceforth the Joint Commission) a vehicle for involving the U.S. government more directly in major development projects, from recommending firms to overseeing contract performance.

The United States, on the other hand, preferred greater government–to–private contractor orientation just as it had with military projects. At a press conference in Riyadh in February 1975, Treasury Secretary Simon stated, "It is our strong conviction that the U.S. private sector is the key element in our participation in Saudi economic development."[86] Over the years since the creation of the Joint Commission, U.S. participation has tilted more in the direction of the Saudi view, though to some degree—under the Reagan administration—it has tilted back.[87]

On the U.S. side, placement of administrative responsibilities for the Joint Commission in the Treasury Department had the disadvantage of Treasury's having little experience in creating and managing a foreign technical assistance program. This appeared to be more than outweighed, however, by the advantages of a fresh start by a highly motivated staff less encumbered with the regulations and procedures binding the Agency for International Development (AID). Moreover, since the costs were fully reimbursable by the Saudi Arabian government, Joint Commission activities were not unduly exposed to the scrutiny and political pressures of the Office of Management and Budget and of congressional oversight.[88]

Operations under the Joint Commission got under way when representatives of the two countries signed a Technical Cooperation Agreement on February 13, 1975. Valid for five years, it was extended in November 1979 for five more years until February 1985. The agreement basically called for

- The United States to provide professional and technical advisors for Saudi economic and human-resources development;
- Both countries to adopt mutually acceptable organizational arrangements;
- The United States, on Saudi request, to prepare studies for specific development projects and to provide advisors for them in accordance with agreed-upon cost estimates; the Saudi government to establish a dollar trust account in the U.S. Treasury and to provide in advance

the full amount of funds necessary to cover the costs of studies and services; and

- The United States to assign administrative support and staff personnel to Saudi Arabia to carry out the purposes of the agreement; and Saudi Arabia to defray all costs.[89]

The fact that U.S. expenditures under the Joint Committee were reimbursable by Saudi Arabia did not entirely prevent it from coming under the scrutiny of the Congress. In 1978 and again in 1983, the comptroller general of the United States was requested by Congressman Lee Hamilton, chairman of the Subcommittee on Europe and the Middle East of the House Committee on Foreign Affairs, to assess the Joint Commission. The resulting GAO reports were, on balance, quite positive. Recommendations in the 1979 GAO report calling for an improved flow of information from the Joint Commission to the business community and for providing assistance to U.S. business in exploring joint ventures with Saudi firms were adopted by the Treasury Department.[90]

Not all congressional scrutiny was positive, however. Congressman Rosenthal raised the question of whether U.S. employees whose salaries were reimbursed by Saudi Arabia might as a result have divided political loyalties. In 1978, P.L. 95-612 required Treasury to pay U.S. salaries and costs for the Joint Commission from appropriations rather than from its own Exchange Stabilization Fund prior to reimbursement. This gave the Congress additional oversight powers. Nevertheless, Rosenthal, in 1981 and 1982, asked the General Accounting Office to look into all reimbursable U.S. programs in Saudi Arabia (the Joint Commission, the U.S. Army Corps of Engineers, and the U.S. Geological Survey of the Department of Interior) and to discuss the legality and constitutionality of reimbursable programs. (It was an ironic twist considering that the Congress is generally more interested in how U.S. taxpayers' dollars are spent than in how foreign funds are spent.) The GAO concluded that none of the programs were in violation of the Constitution or the law.[91]

In its first decade, the U.S.-Saudi Joint Commission has posted a solid record of achievement, particularly in comparison with the other six joint commissions, established about the same time. As of November 1982, eleven U.S. departments and agencies have been involved in twenty-four projects, four of which have been completed, at a total estimated cost of $716.17 million. For the United States, about $350 million in procurements have been awarded to U.S. firms as a direct outgrowth of U.S. involvement in the Joint Commission. Although these figures are perhaps modest in comparison to the billions of dollars spent on Saudi development, the value of the Joint Commission to both countries has been far more qualitative than quantitative. The personal relationships among counterparts, from the U.S. secretary of treasury and the Saudi minister of finance and national economy on down, has been an incalculable boon to close U.S.-Saudi economic and commercial relations.

Economic and Commercial Relations in the Mid-1980s

By the mid-1980s, the world recession and an absolute increase in energy consumption efficiency had led to a major glut in the world oil market and considerable lessening of Western dependence on OPEC oil. Concomitantly, Saudi Arabia found itself in the ironic position of having a negative cash-flow problem in its current account. The resulting decrease in Saudi economic activity, although it has had a braking effect on U.S.-Saudi economic and commercial relations, has not seriously undermined their major significance. In 1982, U.S. exports of industrial (including military) products to Saudi Arabia exceeded $9 billion, with another $500 million in agricultural products. Over 650 U.S. firms were represented in the Kingdom with some 60,000 American employees and dependents.[92] Excluding the number of Americans working in Saudi Arabia, this volume of trade represents about 350,000 jobs generated in the United States. It is no exaggeration to say, therefore, that even in times of reduced economic and commercial activity, U.S.-Saudi relations in these areas remain of considerable importance. Moreover, as the "gold rush" mentality of the immediate post–1973-1974 energy crisis years recedes, those relations have entered a much more stable and mature period.

Notes

1. Expressed in a State Department memorandum of March 15, 1950, cited in U.S. Department of State, *Foreign Relations of the United States,* vol. 5 (Washington, D.C.: Government Printing Office, 1950), p. 34 (hereafter cited as *FRUS* with volume and date).

2. In more recent times, this fact has been lamented as a competitive disadvantage by some firms competing for contracts in Saudi Arabia.

3. See U.S. Congress, Senate, *Multinational Corporations and United States Foreign Policy; Hearings Before the Subcommittee on Multinational Corporations of the Committee on Foreign Relations,* pts. 7 and 8, 93rd Cong., 2d sess., 1975; pt. 12, 94th Cong., 1st sess., 1975, and pt. 14, 94th Cong., 2d sess., 1976 (Washington, D.C.: Government Printing Office, 1975 and 1976).

4. Aaron David Miller, *Search for Security: Saudi Arabian Oil and American Foreign Policy, 1939–1949* (Chapel Hill: University of North Carolina Press, 1980), p. 20.

5. For a discussion of Saudi business ethics, see David E. Long, *Saudi Arabia,* the Washington Papers 4, no. 39 (Beverly Hills, Calif., and London: Sage Publications, 1976), pp. 54–56; and John A. Shaw and David E. Long, *Saudi Arabian Modernization: The Impact of Change on Stability,* the Washington Papers 10, no. 89 (New York: Praeger Publications, 1982), pp. 49–55.

6. David Holden and Richard Johns, *The House of Saud* (London: Sidgwick and Jackson, 1981), pp. 156–157. See also "The Story of Saudi Arabian Airlines" (Jidda, Saudi Arabian Airlines, 1970).

7. Holden and Johns, *The House of Saud,* pp. 156–157.

8. For a discussion of U.S. arms sales to Saudi Arabia, see Chapter 2.

9. U.S. Congress, Senate, *Petroleum Arrangements with Saudi Arabia,* hearings before a Special Committee Investigating the National Defense Program, pt. 41, 80th Cong., 1st sess., 1948 (Washington, D.C.: Government Printing Office, 1948), p. 24804, quoted in Miller, *Search for Security,* p. 36. See also David Sidney Painter, "The Politics of Oil: Multinational Oil Corporations and United States Foreign Policy, 1941–1954" (Ph.D. dissertation, University of North Carolina at Chapel Hill, 1982), pp. 96–97.

10. Miller, *Search for Security.*

11. Painter, "The Politics of Oil," p. 97.

12. Ibid.

13. *FRUS,* vol. 3, 1941, pp. 634–635.

14. Herbert Feis, *Seen From E.A.: Three International Episodes* (New York: Alfred A. Knopf, 1947), p. 129.

15. Miller, *Search for Security,* p. 69.

16. Kirk to secretary of state, January 18, 1941, *FRUS,* vol. 4, 1943, pp. 856–857, quoted in Miller, *Search for Security,* p. 67. Kirk, who was concurrently accredited to Egypt, was resident in Cairo.

17. *FRUS,* vol. 4, 1943, pp. 854–855, 859.

18. During the poverty-stricken years of the 1930s, it is said that Abd al-Aziz's finance minister, Abdallah Sulayman, kept track of the finances of the Kingdom in a big black ledger that he kept under his bed.

19. *FRUS,* vol. 5, 1950, p. 1036.

20. Ibid., p. 1031.

21. See Arthur N. Young, "Economic Review: Saudi Arabian Currency and Finance," pt. 1, *Middle East Journal* 7, no. 3 (1953), p. 362.

22. Saudi Arabia, Royal Decree No. 30/4/1/1047 of 25 Rajab A.H. 1371, corresponding to April 20, 1952, quoted in ibid., p. 379.

23. Arthur N. Young, "Economic Review: Saudi Arabian Currency and Finance," pt. 2, *Middle East Journal* 7, no. 4 (1953), pp. 546–547.

24. *International Financial News Survey,* quoted in ibid., p. 547.

25. Norman C. Walpole et al., *Area Handbook for Saudi Arabia,* American University Foreign Area Studies series (Washington, D.C.: Government Printing Office, 1971), p. 292.

26. Ibid., p. xxxiv.

27. Ibid., p. 292.

28. Statement by Joseph J. Sisco, assistant secretary of state for near eastern and south Asian affairs to the Subcommittee on the Near East and South Asia

of the House Committee on Foreign Affairs, June 6, 1973, Department of State *Bulletin,* July 2, 1973, p. 31.

29. Department of State *Bulletin,* September 2, 1974, p. 336.

30. Ibid.

31. See Richard D. Erb, "Saudi Economic Developments," in Richard D. Erb, ed., "The Arab Oil-Producing States of the Gulf," *AEI Foreign Policy and Defense Review* 2, nos. 3 and 4 (1980), p. 23; David E. Long, *The Persian Gulf: An Introduction to Its Peoples, Politics, and Economics,* rev. ed. (Boulder, Colo.: Westview Press, 1978), p. 153.

32. See Dankwart Rustow, "U.S.-Saudi Relations and the Oil Crisis of the 1980s," *Foreign Affairs* 55, no. 3 (April 1977), p. 497.

33. Statement by J. Dexter Peach, director, Energy and Minerals Division, Department of Treasury, in U.S. Congress, House of Representatives, Committee on Government Operations, hearings before the Subcommittee on Commerce, Consumer, and Monetary Affairs, *The Operations of Federal Agencies in Monitoring, Reporting on, and Analyzing Foreign Investments in the United States* (pt. 2—*OPEC Investment in the United States*), 96th Cong., 1st sess., July 16, 17, 18, and 26, 1979 (Washington, D.C.: Government Printing Office, 1979), pp. 2–3.

34. Ibid., p. 11.

35. U.S. Congress, House of Representatives, *The Operations of Federal Agencies in Monitoring, Reporting on, and Analyzing Foreign Investments in the United States* (pt. 5—*Appendices*), 96th Cong., 1st sess., September 19, 20, 21, 1978; July 16, 17, 18, 26, 30, and 31, and August 1, 1979 (Washington, D.C.: Government Printing Office, 1980), p. 193. This arrangement is open to any country that desires it.

36. Ibid., p. 4.

37. U.S. Congress, House of Representatives, Committee on Government Operations, Subcommittee on Commerce, Consumer, and Monetary Affairs, *Federal Response to OPEC Country Investments in the United States* (pt. 2—*Investment in Sensitive Sectors of U.S. Economy: Kuwait Petroleum Corporation Takeover of Santa Fe International Corporation*), 97th Cong., 1st sess., October 20 and 22, November 24, and December 9, 1981 (Washington, D.C.: Government Printing Office, 1982), p. 5.

38. U.S. Congress, House of Representatives, *The Operations of Federal Agencies,* pt. 5, p. 55.

39. U.S. Congress, House of Representatives, *The Operations of Federal Agencies,* pt. 2, p. 2.

40. See U.S. Congress, Senate, *Multinational Corporations.*

41. U.S. Congress, House of Representatives, *The Operations of Federal Agencies,* pt. 5, pp. 66–69.

42. See U.S. Congress, House of Representatives, *The Operations of Federal Agencies,* pts. 2 and 5; and U.S. Congress, House of Representatives, *Federal Response.*

43. U.S. Congress, House of Representatives, *The Operations of Federal Agencies,* pt. 2, p. 287.

44. See, for example, U.S. Congress, House of Representatives, Committee on Government Operations, Subcommittee on Commerce, Consumer, and Monetary Affairs, *Federal Response to OPEC Country Investments in the United States* (pt. 3—*Saudi Arabian Influence on the Whittaker Corporation*), 97th Cong., 2d sess., April 6, 1982 (Washington, D.C.: Government Printing Office, 1982).

45. U.S. Congress, House of Representatives, *The Operations of Federal Agencies,* pt. 2, p. 290.

46. They included the editor of a little-known technical journal from London, the *International Currency Review,* which had earlier come to outside attention for an exposé on an alleged Saudi "coup" and an alleged U.S.-Saudi "secret agreement" to swap nonmarketable U.S. securities for oil, arms, and developmental assistance. See U.S. Congress, House of Representatives, Committee on Government Operations, Subcommittee on Commerce, Consumer, and Monetary Affairs, *Federal Response to OPEC Country Investments in the United States* (pt. 1—*Overview*), 97th Cong., 1st sess., 1981 (Washington, D.C.: Government Printing Office, 1981), pp. 25–121; and U.S. Congress, House of Representatives, *The Operations of Federal Agencies,* pt. 5, p. 147.

47. U.S. Congress, House of Representatives, *Federal Response,* pt. 1, pp. 27–28.

48. U.S. Congress, House of Representatives, *The Operations of Federal Agencies,* pt. 5, p. 199.

49. Ibid.

50. Ibid., pp. 206–215.

51. U.S. Congress, House of Representatives, *The Operations of Federal Agencies,* pt. 2, pp. 60–69.

52. U.S. Congress, House of Representatives, *The Operations of Federal Agencies,* pt. 5, p. 221.

53. Long, *The Persian Gulf: An Introduction,* p. 153.

54. Nancy Turck, "The Arab Boycott of Israel," *Foreign Affairs* 55, no. 3. (April 1977), p. 485.

55. *New York Times,* January 11, 1977, p. 41.

56. Turck, "The Arab Boycott," pp. 486–487.

57. Ibid.

58. U.S. Department of Commerce, International Trade Administration, Office of Antiboycott Compliance, "Restrictive Trade Practices or Boycotts Including Enforcement in Administrative Proceedings," reprinted from *Export Administrative Regulations* (Washington, D.C.: Government Printing Office, 1983).

59. Ibid., p. iii.

60. Andreas F. Lowenfeld, "Sauce for the Gander . . . The Arab Boycott and United States Political Trade Controls," *Texas International Law Journal* 12, no. 1 (1977), cited in Turck, "The Arab Boycott," p. 483.

61. Ibid., p. 482.

62. *Commerce America,* February 27, 1978, p. 4, quoted in Cexec, Inc., *Saudi Arabia: A Report Submitted to the Department of Energy,* vol. 2, appendices (McLean, Va.: Cexec, Inc., February 15, 1981), p. E-6.

63. Ibid., p. E-11, based on a Chase Econometrics Study, June 1980.

64. Ibid., p. E-13.

65. I was present on several occasions when the U.S. businessmen presented their views.

66. U.S. military and civilian government employees have never been exempt from taxes on income earned abroad, which made them (prior to the 1970s and again after 1982) often the only "American taxpaying citizens" working in Saudi Arabia.

67. P.L. 97-34, 95 Stat., 190 and 196.

68. Cexec, Inc., *Saudi Arabia,* p. E-17.

69. Abdallah T. Dabbagh, "Saudi-U.S. Economic and Commercial Relations," in Ragaei El Mallakh and Dorothea H. El Mallakh, eds., *Saudi Arabia: Energy, Developmental Planning and Industrialization* (Lexington, Mass., and Toronto: Lexington Books, 1982), p. 157.

70. Erb, "Saudi Economic Developments," p. 22.

71. Ibid., p. 23; Shaw and Long, *Saudi Arabian Modernization,* p. 12.

72. Dabbagh, "Saudi-U.S. Economic and Commercial Relations," p. 158.

73. Erb, "Saudi Economic Developments," p. 23.

74. David E. Long, "Saudi Oil Policy," *Wilson Quarterly* 3 (Winter 1979), p. 91.

75. Erb, "Saudi Economic Developments," p. 23.

76. Switzerland in particular had imposed negative interest rates to limit the flow of foreign capital that was driving up its exchange rates. See U.S. Congress, House of Representatives, *The Operations of Federal Agencies,* pt. 2, p. 282.

77. *Arab World,* June 7, 1974, p. 12.

78. U.S. Congress, Senate, *Multinational Corporations,* p. 154, quoted in Holden and Johns, *The House of Saud,* p. 357.

79. Steven Hayes has developed the thesis that the realization of economic interdependence was a major determinant for the U.S. search for economic cooperation following the energy crisis. See Steven D. Hayes, "Joint Economic Commissions as Instruments of U.S. Foreign Policy in the Middle East," *Middle East Journal,* 31, no. 1 (Winter 1977), p. 23.

80. Walter H. Donaldson, "Challenges of an Interdependent World," Department of State *Bulletin,* March 25, 1974, p. 289, quoted in Hayes, "Joint Economic Commissions," p. 17.

81. Jean R. Tartter, "Joint Commissions of the Middle East and India," a case study written for the Senior Seminar in Foreign Policy of the Foreign Service Institute of the Department of State, 18th sess., 1975-1976, p. 13. The embassy anticipated an end to the Arab oil boycott, which did not occur until March 18.

82. *New York Times,* April 6, 1974, cited in "Chronology," *Middle East Journal* 27, no. 3 (Summer 1974), p. 296.

83. For the text of the statement, see *Middle East Journal* 38, no. 3 (Summer 1979), pp. 305–307.

84. Hayes, "Joint Economic Commissions," p. 25.

85. See U.S. Congress, House of Representatives, *The Operations of Federal Agencies,* pt. 5, p. 147 ff.; for U.S. policy on securing oil supplies, see Chapter 2.

86. Tartter, "Joint Commissions," p. 14.

87. Ibid., p. 15.

88. Ibid.

89. U.S. General Accounting Office, *The U.S.–Saudi Arabian Joint Commission on Economic Cooperation,* report by the comptroller of the United States, March 22, 1979 (ID-79-7) (Washington, D.C.: General Accounting Office, 1979), pp. 1–2.

90. See U.S. General Accounting Office, *Status of U.S.–Saudi Arabian Joint Commission on Economic Cooperation,* report by the comptroller general of the United States to the chairman, Subcommittee on Europe and the Middle East, Committee on Foreign Affairs, House of Representatives, May 26, 1983 (GAO/ID-83-32) (Washington, D.C.: General Accounting Office, 1983).

91. U.S. General Accounting Office, *Reimbursement of Federal Employees' Salaries and Benefits by Saudi Arabia,* report to the chairman, Subcommittee on Commerce, Consumer, and Monetary Affairs, Committee on Government Operations, House of Representatives, October 21, 1982 (GAO/ID-83-4) (Washington, D.C.: General Accounting Office, 1982).

92. U.S. Embassy, Jidda, "Directory of American Firms in Saudi Arabia," 1983, pp. 10, 12.

5
U.S.-Saudi Political Relations

Politics runs through the entire gamut of U.S.-Saudi relations, from oil to economics. The issues reserved for discussion in this chapter are more or less limited to regional political issues, diplomatic relations, and those aspects of oil, strategic, and economic concerns that have independent political significance.

From Recognition to Representation: 1931–1940

The United States formally recognized the regime of King Abd al-Aziz (Ibn Saud) in May 1931.[1] It was not until later, in September 1932, that Abd al-Aziz formally created the Kingdom of Saudi Arabia. In 1933, Standard Oil Company of California (Socal) obtained the oil concession that subsequently made Saudi Arabia the world's greatest oil exporter. Even before the concession was signed, Socal had raised with the State Department the question of diplomatic representation.[2] On November 7, 1933, the United States and Saudi Arabia signed a provisional agreement "in regard to diplomatic representation, juridical protection, commerce and navigation," the first formal act of diplomatic relations.[3] Nevertheless, as Secretary of State Henry L. Stimson had already told Francis Loomis of Socal, the United States had no plans for establishing a diplomatic or consular presence in the Kingdom. Such a step, he said, would "depend upon the character and growth of American interests in the Arabian Kingdom."[4]

The United States essentially held to this position until the end of the decade. In 1937, for example, the State Department dispatched its consul general in Alexandria, Egypt, to Jidda to study the advisability of establishing diplomatic representation in Saudi Arabia. He reported back that U.S. interests at that time still did not warrant official representation.[5]

By late 1939, the United States had begun to reevaluate its position. The clouds of war were already gathering, even in Saudi Arabia where the Germans accredited their envoy in Baghdad to be nonresident ambassador. Both Germany and Japan expressed interest in an oil concession. Moreover, Britain, to whom Washington had traditionally looked as preeminent great power in the region, was becoming increasingly more pressed to maintain its position of primacy. Finally, on August 3, 1939, the U.S. minister to Egypt, Bert Fish, was confirmed as nonresident minister to Saudi Arabia. He presented his credentials to King Abd al-Aziz on February 4, 1940.[6]

Even this move could not be considered a major diplomatic initiative. In terms of staffing and administrative support it cost the United States nothing. All that was required was an occasional visit from Cairo, and U.S. officials were already visiting Saudi Arabia on a fairly regular basis. The move represented a heightened but not yet very great U.S. interest in the Kingdom.

World War II and the Foundations for Close Relations: 1942–1945

As the war spread to the Middle East, U.S. interests in Saudi Arabia increased. Strategic military and oil considerations were the catalyst for the establishment of closer political relations; throughout the war years, those relations continued to grow. On May 1, 1942, the United States opened a legation in Jidda. The U.S. minister to Egypt, Alexander Kirk, continued to be the nonresident envoy to Saudi Arabia, and James Moose was appointed resident chargé d'affaires, with the rank of second secretary and consul. Moose was one of the small group of prewar State Department Middle East specialists, having been assigned to Paris in 1930 to learn Arabic and to study the region. In 1943, Moose was appointed resident U.S. minister.[7]

From May to December 1942, a U.S. agricultural mission traveled ten thousand miles throughout the Kingdom conducting an agricultural survey. It was led by Karl Twitchell, an engineer who had surveyed Saudi water resources in the 1930s and had been instrumental in helping Socal obtain its oil concession. The mission, requested by the Saudis, was an early example of the growing U.S. desire to be responsive to King Abd al-Aziz, who was highly appreciative.[8]

In 1943, overall U.S.-Saudi relations were placed on a firmer footing when the United States declared Saudi Arabia to be eligible for Lend-Lease assistance. The resulting aid program was theoretically part of a joint Anglo-American effort to maintain political and economic stability in the Kingdom. By the war's end, the United States had expended nearly $100 million in various forms of aid, of which $72 million was considered nonrecoverable.[9] When Prince (later King) Faysal visited the United States in the fall of 1943 and again in February 1944, he was purposely received in a grand manner calculated to underscore the growing importance of U.S.-Saudi relations.[10]

The United States' new forward policy toward Saudi Arabia raised a broader issue of the necessity for realigning U.S. relations with Great Britain throughout the Middle East. The British, with imperial interests east of Suez, had long assumed primary responsibility for political and economic stability in the region, a role the United States had been perfectly willing to support. Thus, when Casoc and its owners had asked the U.S. government to extend financial assistance to King Abd al-Aziz in 1941, President Roosevelt had asked that Britain "take care of the King of Saudi Arabia. This is a little far afield for us."[11]

Even the U.S. military considered Saudi Arabia to be within the British area of responsibility. The War Department, in its desire to facilitate ferrying aircraft between Karachi and Khartoum, proposed that any agreement for the use of Saudi facilities or airfields be made by the British. In the spring of 1942, Under Secretary of State Sumner Welles, seeing the political advantages of a U.S.-built and operated airfield at Dhahran, was actually out in front of the War Department in suggesting that it be solely a U.S. project.[12]

By 1943, the idea of playing a role independent of the British had begun to gather momentum. In June 1943, Moose was instructed to inform the British minister to Saudi Arabia, Stanley R. Jordan, that the Saudis would deal directly with the United States on the matter of arms sales rather than going through the British as had formerly been the case.[13] Anglo-American cooperation in Saudi Arabia suffered, particularly in military assistance, as rivalry between the two allies increased. One example was the lack of agreement on the joint Anglo-American military training mission in 1944 (discussed in Chapter 3). Another was the U.S.-British military rivalry that reached a peak in October 1944 when the U.S. minister, Colonel William A. Eddy, learned that the British had been involved in the Saudi refusal to allow the United States to build a military airfield at Dhahran. In the face of a vigorous protest from Washington, the British retreated, and in the late months of the war, the United States did build an air strip at Dhahran that was to become the nucleus for the Dhahran air base.[14]

Anglo-American rivalry was not limited to military affairs. Indeed, the central issue was oil. During the war years, U.S. proved reserves were declining at a rate faster than new reserves were being discovered. Washington worried about the possibility that, unless the trend were reversed, the United States would become a net importer of oil. To stave off such an eventuality, U.S. policymakers began to concentrate on the strategic importance of husbanding U.S. oil by using Middle East oil. In this context, the United States viewed with growing concern what it perceived to be British attempts to use the economic assistance it had been giving the Kingdom (in part at U.S. behest) to obtain oil concessions or concessionary terms of supply.

The notion that Britain was consciously trying to further its oil interests in Saudi Arabia at the expense of the United States was also held by Casoc and its owner companies. They found sympathetic ears in the Division of Near Eastern Affairs of the State Department, which shared their views of the importance of protecting the U.S. stake in Saudi oil from British preemption. Indeed, this view became a key factor in the U.S. decision to grant Lend-Lease eligibility to Saudi Arabia in 1943.[15]

Psychological and personality factors also affected the rivalry. It was difficult for the British, accustomed to political paramountcy in the Gulf and the Indian Ocean, to accept the rapidly expanding influence of the United States in Saudi Arabia. Washington, for its part, had its Anglophobes. Among them was Harold Ickes, secretary of the interior and petroleum administrator for war, whose suspicion of British imperial motives "was of the congenital variety common to so many Midwesterners of his and previous generations."[16] Others critical of U.S. deference to the British in the Middle East included James M. Landis, dean of the Harvard Law School (who was serving as U.S. director of economic operations in the Middle East), Senator Henry Cabot Lodge, Jr., and, of course, the State Department "Arabists."[17]

For the most part, the British and Americans in London and Washington, from Winston Churchill and Franklin Roosevelt down, took a broader view of bilateral relations, mutually appreciating the need for cooperation. In the field, however, it was somewhat a different matter. Moose and his British counterpart, Stanley Jordan, drifted into a personality clash as well as a policy conflict. Despite Moose's excellent training and experience as a Middle East specialist, Jordan shared the British Foreign Office view that Moose was "only a second-rank diplomat who spoke little Arabic."[18] Jordan himself was described by Sir Maurice Peterson, the British under secretary of state for foreign affairs, as a "big breezy Australian." He had served in Jidda in the 1920s and apparently saw his role as the self-appointed defender of British imperial interest in Saudi Arabia. Returning to Jidda as British minister in 1943, he was well liked by King Abd al-Aziz and his court.[19]

Less popular in Riyadh was Jordan's attempt to reform Saudi finances. Moose initially applauded Jordan's apparently sincere effort to get the Saudis to rein in their spending habits (particularly with British-provided funds), but he quickly observed that Jordan was also attempting through his reform recommendations to replace U.S. with British influence in Riyadh. When it appeared that Jordan had had a hand in the Saudi decision to sack Najib Salha, the director of mines and public works in the Ministry of Finance and an advocate of closer U.S.-Saudi relations, Moose complained to Washington, which in turn complained to London.[20] The British, thus tweaked, sniffed back, "American impulsiveness and inexperience in dealing with Arabs may sometimes lead them to act injudiciously, but we must endeavor to persuade and guide them on the right lines and be patient with their mistakes."[21] In any event, the Saudis apparently enjoyed the Moose-Jordan rivalry, for it enabled them to play one side off against the other in their ongoing quest for financial and political security.

Moose was recalled in August 1944 and Jordan the following January. The new U.S. minister, Colonel William A. Eddy, numbered among that remarkable group of U.S. missionary children that became the backbone of U.S. government area specialists during and after World War II. Eddy was the son and grandson of Presbyterian missionaries to Lebanon. He had grown up in the Arab world, was fluent in Arabic, and was understanding of Arab culture and behavior. Between 1941 and 1943, he had served as naval attaché in Cairo and chief of the Office of Strategic Services (OSS) in North Africa, before being assigned as a special assistant to Moose in January 1944. Although Anglo-American rivalry continued briefly following his appointment, it ultimately abated as the U.S. position in the Kingdom solidified and Britain turned to more pressing postwar problems in the Middle East.

The turning point of U.S.-Saudi political relations during this period was the famous visit of King Abd al-Aziz with President Roosevelt aboard the USS *Quincy* in the Great Bitter Lake on February 14, 1945. The president was returning from Yalta and arranged to meet Abd al-Aziz, whose support he wished to solicit in seeking a solution to the Palestine problem.[22]

Roosevelt had always been ambivalent about the Palestine issue, originally believing it to be a British and not a U.S. problem. As the horrors of the Nazi holocaust had become fully known, however, he had expressed support for Jewish immigration to Palestine and had endorsed the idea of a homeland for the Jewish people. On the other hand, he was also aware of the threat to U.S. interests in the Middle East that would result in supporting a Jewish homeland over the solid and fervent opposition of the Arabs. Thus in May 1943, Roosevelt wrote Abd al-Aziz, then considered the most prominent leader of an Arab state wholly independent of Western imperial constraints, and promised him that no U.S. government decision would be made altering the basic situation in Palestine without full prior consultation with both Arabs and Jews.[23]

In midsummer 1943, Roosevelt had sent Lieutenant Colonel Harold Hoskins to Saudi Arabia to determine whether the king would discuss with Dr. Chaim Weizmann or other Jewish Agency representatives a solution of the Palestine problem.[24] King Abd al-Aziz was unalterably opposed to a Jewish state in Palestine and refused to discuss it with Weizmann or anyone else. The king appeared to view the problem more in terms of abstract justice than operational politics and felt it was up to British and the United States to arrive at a just solution.

At the historic meeting aboard the USS *Quincy,* Abd al-Aziz was apparently an able spokesman for the Arab point of view on the Palestine issue. Colonal Eddy, who served as interpreter, also played a role in making the meeting a success. There is no doubt that Roosevelt was charmed by the desert king; critics in the United States, mainly supporters of Jewish immigration to Palestine, would say the president was taken in by him.[25] Nevertheless, Roosevelt subseqently informed the Congress in an address on March 1, 1945, that "from Ibn Saud of Arabia, I learned more of the whole problem of the Muslims and about the Jewish problem that I could have learned by the exchange of a dozen letters."[26] Roosevelt also reaffirmed to Abd al-Aziz that he personally would never do anything that might prove hostile to the Arabs and that the United States would not act on the Palestine problem without consulting both Arabs and Jews. This pledge was again reaffirmed in a letter to the king in April, one of the last Roosevelt ever wrote.[27]

Postwar Relations: 1945–1953

The strategic concerns that had been the major determinants of political relations during World War II began to wane in the postwar era. To be sure, the threat of a U.S. domestic oil shortage continued for several years; and, in 1948, the United States briefly became a net oil importer for the first time. Moreover, the European Recovery Program (the official name of the Marshall Plan) became increasingly dependent on Middle East oil. Nevertheless, by the 1950s, the world oil market had again reverted to a glut and a buyers' market (see Chapter 2), lessening considerably direct U.S. strategic concern over threats to the availability of Saudi oil.

At the same time, two developments occurred in the immediate postwar period that were to become primary determinants of U.S.-Saudi political relations and—taken together—the primary cause of ambivalence in those relations up to the present time. They were the advent of the cold war and the creation of the State of Israel.

The postwar Soviet threat in the Middle East created a mutual U.S.-Saudi security interest that has been the backbone of political relations for almost forty years. In March 1947, the Truman Doctrine, by which the United States took over from Britain the responsibility for maintaining security in the eastern Mediterranean and the Middle East, established a long-term U.S. global policy for containing communism that has generally coincided with Saudi security interests. For the most part these mutual security interests have enabled the two countries to surmount differences and opposing interests and to maintain close and friendly relations over the years.

The major difference has been over the Arab-Israel problem ever since the creation of Israel in 1948. It is doubtful whether President Roosevelt, given the pressures of U.S. domestic politics, could have found a solution to the Palestine problem acceptable to Abd al-Aziz (or, indeed, to any Arab), despite Roosevelt's empathy with the king and his appreciation of the threat to U.S. Middle East interests certain to be incurred by the creation of a Jewish state in Palestine. President Truman, however, took even less account of Arab sensibilities, reportedly dismissing the counsel of the State Department on possible damage to U.S. prestige with the retort, "I'm sorry, gentlemen, but I have to answer to hundreds of thousands who are anxious for the success of Zionism. I do not have hundreds of thousands of Arabs among my constituents."[28]

When the United States voted in the United Nations for partition of Palestine in 1947, the Saudis felt that President Harry S Truman had personally betrayed the promises made to them by his predecessor. The king's son and foreign minister, Prince (later King) Faysal, felt particularly bitter, having been assured by the State Department during a visit to Washington in 1946 that Roosevelt's assurances were still in effect. After the United Nations vote on November 30, 1947, to partition Palestine, the announcement of the creation of Israel on May 15, 1948, and U.S. recognition of it, Faysal urged his father to break diplomatic relations with the United States.[29] Truman, on the other hand, denied that he had any hostile intent toward the Arabs and expressed the hope that Abd al-Aziz would use his prestige and influence to work toward a just and lasting solution.[30]

Despite Saudi bitterness over the U.S. role in the creation of Israel, U.S.-Saudi relations continued to expand. The American Consulate in Dhahran was raised to a Consulate General in 1949, followed by the American Legation's in Jidda being raised to an embassy. The U.S. minister, J. Rives Childs, became the first U.S. ambassador.[31]

The Saud-Eisenhower Years: 1953–1960

The reign of King Saud bin Abd al-Aziz Al Saud (1953–1964) coincided to a great degree with Eisenhower's years as president (1952–1960).

Although Saud remained king four years after Eisenhower left office, he was king in name only for the last two years of his reign. It was the Eisenhower administration, therefore, that dealt most closely with King Saud.

From the beginning, that administration involved itself far more intensively with the Arab world than had its predecessor, a course that led to its role in the creation of the Baghdad Pact in 1955, the mediation of the Suez crisis in 1956, and the Eisenhower Doctrine of 1957. This involvement, however, caused a decidedly mixed reaction among the Arab states, particularly Saudi Arabia. Much of the cause can be attributed to different and often conflicting perceptions of mutual interests. The 1950s witnessed the height of the cold war, and the United States viewed Arab politics primarily as an adjunct of global politics. Containing Communist expansion was the primary U.S. political goal in the Middle East, and Washington's insensitivity to local and regional political issues was greatly to complicate its relations with Arab states.

Saudi Arabia, on the other hand, although still concerned over the Communist threat, was also concerned about a perceived threat from the Hashimite kingdoms of Jordan and Iraq. Their rulers descended from King Husayn of the Hijaz (the former sharif of Makkah) who had been deposed by Abd al-Aziz in the 1920s. Saudi concern over the Hashimites caused King Saud to become enmeshed in Arab politics in which Egypt and Iraq were vying for leadership of the Arab world. It also set Saudi Arabia at odds with Great Britain, the former mandatory power over both Iraq and Jordan and still their close ally. British-Saudi relations deteriorated further as a result of the Saudi territorial dispute over the Buraymi Oasis with the British-protected Oman and Trucial States (now the United Arab Emirates) and of Saudi support for the imam of Oman who, in 1955, was defeated by British troops for challenging the authority of the Omani sultan.

To the United States, all these concerns appeared largely trivial, to be quickly mediated when they could not be altogether ignored. The Saudis responded to this attitude with increasing resentment. The resulting series of misperceptions, unrealistic expectations, and insensitivity of the interests of the other led to a prolonged period of strain and ambivalence in U.S.-Saudi political relations.

The Baghdad Pact

From the beginning of the cold war in the late 1940s, the United States had sought security arrangements in the region, including the use of the Dhahran airfield. The primary focus of Secretary of State John Foster Dulles was on the "Northern Tier" states bordering the Soviet Union: Turkey, Iran, and Pakistan. The United States wished to secure the participation of the Arab states, together with the Northern Tier states, in a defense pact to be called the Middle East Defense Organization (MEDO). In December 1953, Saud stated his unequivocal opposition to MEDO, and in March 1954, he went to Cairo to seek President Nasser's support in opposing the Arab–Northern Tier alliance.[32] The resulting Saudi-Egyptian military alliance was more a political than a military gesture.[33]

The Americans dropped the MEDO idea, but the British, who were initially chary of MEDO, pressed on, feeling the need for a multilateral pact to supersede their bilateral defense pact with Iraq. Secretary of State Dulles assented, and in 1955 the Baghdad Pact was formed. The United States did not become a full member of the Baghdad Pact, although in fact it was a full participant. Among the reasons for not becoming a formal member was Dulles's apparent belief that if the United States were not a signatory, Egyptian and also Saudi qualms could be overcome. It was not to be. Nasser felt that he had been betrayed, claiming that Britain and the United States made a "gentlemen's agreement" to postpone any such pact; he and Saud saw their rival, Iraq, in a position to claim leadership of the entire Arab world. Thus, the Baghdad Pact split the Arab world, drew conservative Saudi Arabia into an unnatural alliance with revolutionary Egypt, and also threatened to undermine U.S.-Saudi political relations.

Creation of the Baghdad Pact also further estranged the Saudis and the British and indirectly placed extra strains on U.S.-British relations as well, strains that stemmed from more than the United States' "coming of age" and the overall decline of British influence in the region. The United States, despite heightened tensions in its relations with Saudi Arabia and despite British sensitivities, still independently sought Saudi friendship. Indeed, as U.S.-Egyptian relations deteriorated, the Eisenhower administration entertained the notion of building up King Saud as a conservative, spiritual leader, to counter the growing Pan-Arab influence of President Nasser.[34]

The Buraymi Oasis Dispute

Another major irritant in U.S.-British relations involving Saudi Arabia centered around the territorial dispute over the Buraymi Oasis, located on the Saudi–Abu Dhabi–Omani frontier. The Saudis had occupied the oasis in the early nineteenth century and converted some of the tribes to the Wahhabi Islamic revival movement. They had withdrawn in 1869 during a period of Saudi political decline but had never relinquished their claim. As in most of the Arabian Peninsula in those days, tribal allegiance more than geographical borders determined sovereignty. Following the Saudi withdrawal, the region fell under the spheres of the shaykh of Abu Dhabi and the sultan of Muscat (Oman), who in turn came under the protection of the British. The territorial dispute remained relatively quiescent for years, until Aramco oil exploration in the vicinity of the oasis in 1949 prompted the Saudis again to press their claim to Buraymi. With possible oil discoveries at stake, the British were quick to defend Abu Dhabi's and Oman's territorial rights, as was Aramco to lend logistic and other support in defense of the Saudi claim. As a U.S. company, Aramco was seen by many Britons as at least a passive instrument of U.S. policies.[35]

Matters became worse in 1952 when a small Saudi force under Turki bin Utayshan occupied one of the oasis villages. U.S. Ambassador Raymond Hare was able to effect a truce among the parties, and Abd al-Aziz thereupon asked the United States to mediate the dispute. Despite the king's urging, Washington did not wish to become further embroiled, and in April 1953, Abd al-Aziz agreed to international arbitration.

The tribunal convened in 1955. Aramco again aided the Saudis, helping to prepare the Saudi case (known as the Saudi Memorial) that was much more detailed than its British counterpart.[36] Whether or not the Saudis had the better case, however, will never be known, for the British withdrew from the proceedings convinced that the Saudis were trying to influence the outcome through bribery. The dispute, as well as the two sides' leading protagonists, quickly fell back into obscurity; when Saudi Arabia and Abu Dhabi resolved the issue in 1974, it scarcely caused a ripple outside the Arabian Peninsula.[37] Nevertheless in 1955, it was a serious, if somewhat petty, irritant between the United States and Great Britain as well as between Britain and Saudi Arabia.

The 1956 Suez Crisis

Of far more importance to U.S.–United Kingdom relations in the Middle East was the rift between the United States on the one side and Britain, France, and Israel on the other in the Suez crisis of 1956. Nasser, unable to purchase arms in the West on terms Egypt could meet, turned to the Soviet bloc and purchased Czech arms in the summer of 1955. The U.S. secretary of state, John Foster Dulles, was infuriated at Nasser's action and his growing neutralism (the Bandung Conference of nonaligned states was held the same year). On July 19, 1956, Dulles peremptorily withdrew a U.S. offer to fund the construction of the Aswan high dam, a move calculated to humble Nasser. Seven days later, Nasser nationalized the Suez Canal, thus setting off the Suez crisis.

Although he had every right to do so under international law, Nasser's act was seen by Britain and France as an infringement of their "rights." It appeared, however, more a question of honor in the face of crumbling colonial empires than one of rights under international law. By October, the question had reached the United Nations (UN) Security Council, but neither Britain nor France was assuaged by steps taken there. More importantly, their enmity toward Egypt created a temporary convergence of interests with Israel, which saw the Sinai Peninsula in terms of strategic depth with which to defend itself and, conversely, as a bargaining chip to coerce Egypt into making peace. In collusion with Britain and France, Israel invaded Sinai on October 29, 1956. On October 30, Britain and France issued an ultimatum to both sides to withdraw ten miles from the Suez Canal and to allow British and French troops to interpose themselves between the antagonists and "protect" the canal. They subsequently rushed troops to the area in an attempt to secure it before a cease-fire could come into effect.

To the apparent surprise of Britain, France, and Israel, the United States took a strong stand in the United Nations opposing the invasions and was ultimately instrumental in pressuring the three nations into accepting a cease-fire (Britain and France on November 6 and Israel, after more coercion, on November 8). Again largely as a result of U.S. pressure, Israel reluctantly withdrew from the Sinai by March 8, 1957.[38]

The Eisenhower Doctrine

Support of Egypt by the United States against its European allies greatly muted the undercurrent of Arab bitterness at the U.S. role in the creation of Israel. It did not, however, alter Dulles's cold war vision of Middle East politics. Alarmed at the breach with Britain, Dulles moved quickly to extend further support to the Baghdad Pact. Moreover, fearing that the Soviets would fill a so-called power vacuum in the Middle East, the United States hastily concocted a policy to counter the Soviet threat. The Eisenhower Doctrine, as it came to be called, was in the form of a joint congressional resolution calling on the president to employ U.S. armed forces, as deemed necessary, to protect the independence and integrity of any Middle East state requesting such aid against overt armed aggression from any state controlled by international communism; to proffer military assistance programs to any state desiring them; and to assist in economic development for the maintenance of national independence and stability.[39]

Despite existing tensions in U.S.-Saudi relations, the United States looked to King Saud as the Arab spokesman to sell the Eisenhower Doctrine to his fellow Arab leaders. Two days after the draft joint resolution was delivered to Congress on January 5, 1957, it was announced that King Saud would pay a state visit to Washington in late January or early February. Although the invitation had been planned long before, the Eisenhower administration's linkage of it and the Eisenhower Doctrine was not lost on the Congress. As the time for the King's visit approached, the Kingdom's critics in the Congress became more vociferous.[40]

During the congressional debate, the administration attempted to show that the new policy was essential to containing Soviet expansionism in the Middle East. The Congress, however, remained skeptical of administration arguments. Dulles told of "desperate appeals" for assurances of U.S. assistance against Soviet attack by regional states, but the countries he cited were already members of the Baghdad Pact.[41] In the case of Saudi Arabia, the Eisenhower Doctrine was found to constitute a less binding U.S. military commitment than that embodied in a presidential letter of October 1950 from President Truman to King Abd al-Aziz.[42] There even appeared to be some confusion among U.S. diplomats about how the new policy would confront the Soviet threat in the region. The U.S. ambassador to Saudi Arabia, George Wadsworth, stated in testimony in support of the Eisenhower Doctrine: "We are recognizing that Saudi Arabia is a stabilizing force in the area, and we state in those terms for the first time to my knowledge, that it is our policy to continue to contribute to the strengthening of the Kingdom; we want to build up something strong which will resist this nebulous force of aggression which we sense building up."[43]

Wadsworth, while dutifully testifying on behalf of the new policy, admitted that the first he had ever heard of it was through United Press and BBC coverage in Jidda.[44] Nevertheless, despite rather more heat than light being generated by the debate, there was really no question of the resolution's failing, and after two months of hearings, it passed both houses of Congress.

The Saudis were also ambivalent about supporting the Eisenhower Doctrine. Saudi reservations over U.S. intentions toward the regime and its policies toward Iraq, Jordan, and Israel were real enough. On the other hand, the Saudis lauded the U.S. role in the Suez crisis, and although they identified with President Nasser's effort to restore honor to the Arabs in their dealings with the West, the Saudis were becoming increasingly more concerned by the leftward drift of Nasser's foreign policy.

It is not entirely clear how much King Saud really understood either Nasser's exploitation of Pan-Arabism or the U.S. single-dimensional attempt to contain communism. At any rate, when the king arrived in Washington on January 30, 1957, Dulles undertook a hard-sell campaign that succeeded in winning not only Saud's endorsement but also his agreement to use persuasion on other Arab heads of state, including not only Nasser but Prince Abd al-Illah, the regent of Iraq. Saudi-Iraqi rapprochement was cemented by the visit to Saudi Arabia of Amir Zaid, Sharif Husayn's apolitical youngest son. The idea of the visit came from Hermann Eilts and was urged on the reluctant Abd al-Illah by U.S. Ambassador Waldemar Gallman and the British ambassador to Iraq.[45] Thus, if the Eisenhower Doctrine did nothing else, it helped to heal the long-standing Hashimite–Al Saud feud. At least part of Saud's cooperativeness, however, apparently came from his hopes of parlaying Saudi agreement for a five-year extension of the Dhahran airfield agreement into tangible U.S. military and economic aid. He succeeded to the amount of $180 million.

U.S. expectations for Saud as a strong conservative counter to Nasser were quickly dashed. Saud was wholly unsuccessful in selling the Eisenhower Doctrine, and his foreign policy behavior became so erratic as to be more of a liability than a benefit to either the United States or Saudi Arabia. Moreover, even the Saudis hesitated to invoke the full brunt of Egyptian invective their close relations with the United States were bringing them, and many Saudis, including Crown Prince Faysal, still retained a certain admiration for Nasser. At any event, Saud was forced to relinquish operational control of the government to Crown Prince Faysal in 1958, ending any hopes the Eisenhower administration had for making Saud a champion of Arab conservatives. By the time Saud regained governmental control in 1960, President Eisenhower's tenure in office was coming to an end.

Nasser, Yemen, and U.S.-Saudi Relations: 1961–1967

President Kennedy's inauguration in January 1961 marked an end to the strident cold war policies of Eisenhower and Dulles. In the Middle East, the United States would try once again to create a rapprochement with Nasser. On the Saudi side, whatever lingering admiration for Nasser there had been among the Saudi leadership had turned to abiding antipathy and apprehension. Not only was Nasser's foreign policy increasingly militant and revolutionary and his invective against the Saudi regime more shrill, but his charismatic appeal to young Saudis was seen as a growing threat to stability. These concerns were reinforced by the self-imposed "exile" of the so-called Free Princes. In August 1962, Princes Tallal, Badr, Fawwaz, and Saud bin Fahd, calling for a democratic political system, broke with the family and moved to Cairo, where they served as an object of embarrassment to Saudi Arabia and of propaganda manipulation for Nasser. As a result of all these events, Saudi Arabia entered a new Arab political alignment of conservative states against the leftist Pan-Arabism of Nasser, his followers, his emulators, and his left-wing rivals.

Saud briefly regained control of the government in 1960 but lost it permanently in 1962. In March of that year, Faysal became deputy prime minister, and in October he gained total control of the government. In 1964, he became king in his own right when Saud was forced to abdicate.

Faysal was altogether a different leader from his ineffectual half-brother. His experience in foreign affairs dated from his fourteenth year, when he visited England and stopped by Versailles during the peace conference. His independence from Western influence first had him labeled a Nasserist and leftist, and later a conservative and reactionary. In fact, Faysal was proud, pious, but also pragmatic. It was clear to him that the monotheistic West was a lesser threat to the Islamic world he hoped to preserve than the atheistic Soviet bloc and its radical clients in the Middle East. He was frustrated at Kennedy's failure to see Nasser as a threat to U.S. Middle East interests and to champion anti-Communist Saudi Arabia and other Arab conservatives.

Another ideological barrier existed between Saudi Arabia and the idealists in the Kennedy administration. Many in the new Kennedy administration viewed social and economic development largely in terms of Western secular, liberal, representative democratic norms. From their perspective, the Kingdom appeared reactionary, corrupt, and out of step with the desires of its "more enlightened" subjects. Social, political, and economic reform was a major theme of the incoming administration in 1961. Indeed, it was President Kennedy's emphasis on reform that at least in part led Faysal to announce a Ten Point Reform Program in November 1962. Public linkage of Saudi reforms and U.S. cooperation, on the other hand, greatly angered the crown prince when a letter to him from Kennedy was leaked to the press in January 1963.[46] Nevertheless, throughout the 1960s, the United States continued, somewhat patronizingly, to urge reform on Saudi Arabia.[47] It is perhaps a mark of Faysal's wisdom that he never succumbed to such wishes, believing that his own evolutionary approach was far more appropriate for conservative Saudi society than the accelerated modernization programs of such neighbors as the shah of Iran.[48]

The outbreak of the Yemeni Civil War in the fall of 1962 made military and security considerations the top priority in U.S.-Saudi relations. On the political side, the civil war was seen by the Americans as a threat to its efforts to maintain good relations with both the Saudis, who supported the Yemeni royalists, and the Egyptians, who supported the republicans. The Saudis were particularly incensed when, on December 19, the United States—having received assurances from President Abdallah Sallal of the Yemen Arab Republic that he would honor existing treaty obligations and from the United Arab Republic that it would withdraw its troops—extended recognition to the Yemen Arab Republic.

The assurances proved worthless. By the end of 1962, the situation in Yemen had deteriorated rapidly. Saudi Arabia became actively engaged in supporting the Yemeni royalists, and the United Arab Republic (UAR—formed by the merger of Egypt and Syria in 1958) became more deeply involved in the war, ultimately sending up to eighty-five thousand troops to Yemen. UAR aircraft bombed the Saudi border towns of Najran and Jizan in December and again in January 1963, and a number of Saudi air force pilots defected to Cairo. In February, the Saudis discovered a parachute drop of arms and explosives, presumably sent by the UAR to be used by antiregime saboteurs.

In response to the growing crisis, the United States dispatched Ambassador Ellsworth Bunker to Saudi Arabia in March 1963 to try to negotiate a Saudi-UAR disengagement in Yemen. Negotiations were spirited. In an effort to break the impasse, President Kennedy sent a message to Faysal urging him to accept Bunker's proposals and to let Bunker try to work out with Nasser an agreement whereby, on a mutually agreed-upon date, Saudi Arabia would suspend aid to the Yemeni royalists and the UAR would begin withdrawal of its troops.

By April, Bunker finally achieved an agreement, but came to nothing. The Bunker Agreement provided for a United Nations observer mission jointly funded by Saudi Arabia and the UAR. The mission entered Yemen in July 1963 and stayed until September 1964. At that time, with no UAR withdrawal and with hostilities unrelenting, Faysal repudiated the Bunker Agreement and flew to Alexandria to negotiate another settlement. This and subsequent efforts also failed, and the Saudi-Egyptian confrontation in Yemen continued until Nasser was forced to pull out his troops as a result of the June 1967 Arab-Israeli war.

The June war radically changed the entire Middle East political landscape. UAR troop withdrawal led to the collapse of the Yemeni Civil War. It was to be three more years, however, before a settlement between the Yemeni royalists and republicans was completed, largely under the aegis of the Saudis. The Yemen Arab Republic remained, but realigned with Saudi Arabia and other conservative Arab states.

Despite the failure of the Bunker Agreement, U.S. responsiveness to Saudi military needs and restored Saudi internal stability following the accession of King Faysal in 1964 led to a considerable improvement in Saudi political relations. Faysal's state visit to the United States on June 21–23, 1966 (Defense Minister Prince Sultan had visited in February), further cemented relations. Indeed, the improved atmosphere was probably an important factor in the Saudi decision not to break relations with the United States following the June war, one of the few Arab states not to do so. Faysal still believed that despite the United States' pro-Israeli policies, it remained the bulwark in the defense of the Muslim and Arab worlds against threats from Communists and their surrogates. Even in the abortive Arab oil embargo following the 1967 war, Faysal quietly allowed shipments of J-9 jet fuel used by the U.S. Air Force in Vietnam.

A Period of Transition: 1967–1973

The years between 1967 and 1973 were politically a period of transition in the Arabian Peninsula. The Nasserist threat that had dominated Saudi foreign and defense policy throughout most of the 1960s abated after 1967 and ended completely with the settlement of the Yemeni Civil War and the death of President Nasser himself in 1970.

Nevertheless political relations continued to be overshadowed by military and regional security considerations. On November 29, 1967, the British withdrew from Aden after 129 years, leaving behind a Marxist regime in South Yemen. Originally called the People's Republic of Southern Yemen (PRSY), the newly independent country was renamed the People's Democratic Republic of Yemen (PDRY). In short order, South Yemen became a major security threat to the entire Arabian Peninsula. It began efforts to undermine the moderate republican regime in North Yemen and to support a Marxist-led insurgency in the neighboring Dhufar Province of Oman. On November 26, 1969, South Yemeni troops attacked an isolated Saudi border post at al-Wadiy'ah.

Saudi Lightnings and F-86s beat off the South Yemeni attackers. They were aided by British contract personnel. At the same time, the United States was asked for noncombat logistic support. Wishing to be responsive but not to give the impression that the Saudis had an open-ended commitment presented the United States with a difficult diplomatic task, particularly in light of Saudi sensitivities over U.S. reliability as a protector. In the flush of the al-Wadiy'ah "victory," such sensitivities quickly receded, but they were a reminder of continuing mutual ambivalence.[49]

On January 17, 1968, the British suddenly announced their intention to withdraw their political and military protection from the Persian Gulf by 1971. The Gulf states, Saudi Arabia, and the United States were all caught off guard, their primary concern being that the Soviets and their radical Arab surrogates would attempt to fill the "vacuum" created by the departing British. The British did try to tidy up the lower Gulf by creating a federation of nine Gulf shaykhdoms. Failing that, they departed, leaving behind the independent states of Bahrain, Qatar, and the United Arab Emirates (the seven former Trucial States).

The United States, which had always looked to the British to maintain security in the vital, oil-rich Gulf, was forced to develop its own Gulf policy. Ultimately called the Two Pillar Policy, it envisaged Saudi Arabia and Iran as the two major U.S. allies in the region. The Two Pillar Policy was essentially a strategic concept (see Chapter 3), and the political ramifications of it were relatively minor until 1973.

The 1967–1973 period of transition came to an abrupt end in the fall and winter with the October 1973 Arab-Israeli war, the two OPEC price hikes that quadrupled the price of oil, and the Saudi-led Arab oil embargo. After the lifting of the embargo, U.S.-Saudi political relations quickly normalized, but the terms of the relationship had shifted greatly. No longer an obscure, often cash-hungry desert kingdom, Saudi Arabia had changed almost overnight into a major oil power.

A Special Relationship: 1973–1980

The "special relationship" between the United States and Saudi Arabia was the product of a long evolutionary process that began long before John Sawhill brought the phrase into vogue in testimony before the Senate hearings on multinational corporations in 1976.[50] For years, U.S. leaders had reiterated the U.S. commitment to the security of Saudi Arabia. In the 1950s and 1960s, briefing books for senior U.S. official visitors to the kingdom regularly included lists of statements reaffirming the U.S. commitments to the security of Saudi Arabia in chronological order, usually beginning with President Roosevelt's pledge to King Abd al-Aziz aboard the USS *Quincy* in 1946.

For the United States, emergence of Saudi Arabia as a major oil power in 1973 greatly increased the desirability of seeking a special relationship. Secretary of State Henry Kissinger saw that special relationship with Saudi Arabia as a means to enlist moderate Arab support for the Arab-Israeli peace process, to insure the uninterrupted flow of oil to the West at reasonable prices, and to promote the sale of U.S. technology and services in order to lessen the adverse balance of payments due to higher oil imports at higher prices.

The Saudis also desired a special relationship. Foremost, as ever, was their concern over security. Saudi Arabia's position as the world's leading oil-exporting country gave it political leverage far out of proportion to its small population and its embryonic defense establishment. The two greatest external threats in Saudi eyes were communism and Zionism. The first was seen as an atheistic ideology that threatened to engulf the Muslim world, the second as a cancer in the midst of the Arab world that, until the Arab-Israeli problem was resolved, would continue to breed frustration and radicalism. In the Saudi view, the United States as a superpower was the only country that could contain Soviet-supported and -inspired radical expansionism; because of its special relationship with Israel, the United States was the only country that could force Israel into the necessary concessions for a truly just peace settlement. The Saudis also wished to be assured of U.S. technology transfers and development assistance in putting their great oil wealth to work in modernizing the country.

Prior to the death of President Nasser in 1970, the Saudis shied away from an active role in Arab politics, unwilling to subjugate themselves to being alternately abused and importuned for financial aid by the radical Arabs. The October 1973 Arab-Israeli war, however, catapulted the Kingdom into the midst of Arab politics. For almost a year before the war, King Faysal had tried to warn the West, particularly the United States, that unless some progress were made on an Arab-Israeli settlement, renewed hostilities were virtually inevitable; in any event, the Arabs would have to consider the oil weapon if the United States did not apply more pressure on Israel to relinquish the occupied Arab territories. To Faysal's extreme frustration, Washington refused to take his warnings seriously.[51]

Short of war, it is difficult to gauge whether Faysal would have in fact resorted to an oil embargo. More his usual style would have been a decision not to increase productive capacity, thus pressuring the West more indirectly. Even during the 1973 war, Faysal hesitated until the United States announced its intention to provide $2.2 billion in arms to Israel. Having been assured by President Nixon that the United States would be "evenhanded" in the war, Faysal felt personally betrayed, much as he had felt personally betrayed by President Truman over the creation of Israel a quarter-century before. On October 17, Faysal, working through the Organization of Arab Petroleum Exporting Countries (OAPEC), declared an oil embargo against the United States and the Netherlands.[52]

Even after the war, the Saudis still did not view themselves as an Arab confrontation state against Israel. In the Saudi tradition, they saw themselves in a more juridical than operational role in the peace process, as final arbiters of whether or not sufficient justice had been achieved for the Palestinian cause. It was Israel, not Saudi Arabia, that viewed the Kingdom as a confrontation state. Having largely ignored Saudi Arabia prior to the energy crisis of 1973, the Israelis increasingly viewed Saudi oil power as potentially a greater threat than the combined capability of all the Arab armed forces.

As Israel adopted a more vocally hostile stance toward Saudi Arabia, the Saudi leadership's long concern over a direct Israeli military threat became even more intense. It feared that the Kingdom could no longer rule out an Israeli preemptive strike. Continuing and gratuitous Israeli military reconnaissance over northwest Saudi Arabia after 1964 reinforced that concern. Moreover, the Saudis believed that the longer the conflict went unresolved, the more radicalized the Arab world was likely to become. Having developed a new sense of urgency to resolve the conflict, Faysal set out to build a strong Arab consensus for peace. He believed that by unifying the Arabs, they would be able to enter peace negotiations from strength and to obtain recognition of Palestinian territorial and political rights, requisite, in the Saudi view, to a final settlement.

Saudi and U.S. interests appeared to coincide in their mutual desire for a peace settlement. U.S. Secretary of State Henry Kissinger, in a spirit of candor and friendship, kept the Saudis informed of his "shuttle diplomacy" to Cairo, Tel Aviv, and Damascus. The Saudi minister of state for foreign affairs, Sayyid Umar Saqqaf, visited Washington in August 1974, and in October, Kissinger visited Riyadh. During departure ceremonies for Secretary Kissinger, Saqqaf declared that his earlier skepticism of Kissinger's peacemaking efforts had been overcome.[53] King Faysal, however, was less sanguine, causing Saqqaf to add in his farewell remarks: "Time has proved that mutual frankness is the only path to friendship and solutions. Dr. Kissinger has heard from His Majesty the King the viewpoint of Saudi Arabia and an explanation of Saudi policy toward world questions and toward the problems of the area. . . . I will continue to strive to explain the details of this policy. . . ."[54]

Faysal was particularly disturbed by the prospect of a Sinai II agreement, which, he feared, would cause a break between Egypt and Syria despite Saudi Arabia's efforts to keep a united Arab front. Faysal's concern was well founded. Syria did indeed break with Egypt when the Sinai II agreement was concluded in September 1975. The agreement also marked the effective end of Kissinger's shuttle diplomacy.

Faysal was not to see the agreement finalized, however, for on March 24, 1975, he was shot and killed by a deranged nephew. At the time of his death, he was the leading statesman in the region and an internationally recognized leader respected by friend and foe alike. With quiet dignity and single-minded determination, he had presided over his country's foreign affairs as its first and virtually only foreign minister (excepting the 1960–1962 period when he retired to private life) since the portfolio was created in 1932. The foreign policies begun by Faysal were continued by his successor, King Khalid, and by Crown Prince Fahd, who took over much of the day-to-day government operations. Indeed, Fahd, more than any other Saudi leader, pursued a special relationship with the United States. He was the driving force for closer military, political, and economic relations. The U.S.-Saudi Joint Commission, for example, was largely his brainchild.

Over the next year, Saudi diplomacy aimed at healing the Egyptian-Syrian rift. Saudi patience paid off, at least temporarily. On October 18, 1976, Egyptian President Anwar Sadat and Syrian President Hafiz al-Assad agreed to attend a mini summit meeting in Riyadh prior to a full summit in Cairo. Together with Palestine Liberation Organization (PLO) leader Yassir Arafat and Lebanese President Ilyas Sarkis, they came to discuss a cease-fire in the Lebanese Civil War.[55] The Saudis were jubilant. Having, in their view, revived the Arab unity, they felt that they could then call on the United States to exert sufficient leverage on Israel to get the sidetracked peace process started again. If fact, the minisummit only papered over Egyptian-Syrian difference.

In January 1977, the Carter administration came into office. Initially, the Saudis were optimistic. Carter sent a personal friend and former governor of South Carolina, John C. West, to be the new U.S. ambassador to Saudi Arabia. To the Saudis' highly personalized perceptions, the appointment guaranteed direct access to the president. Carter, moreover, appeared willing to take on the politically no-win Palestinian problem. On May 11, 1977, Fahd stated that "all Arabs, including Palestinians" were willing to negotiate with Israel if it would recognize the full rights of the Palestinian people.[56] During his May 24–25 visit to Washington, Fahd asked President Carter to urge the Israelis to keep an open mind on a just and lasting peace and expressed "his strong hope that Israel would be reassured about the inclinations of his country toward the protection of their security."[57]

Throughout the summer, the Saudis, working closely with the United States, attempted to get the PLO to modify its maximalist claim to all of old Palestine, so that the PLO could join the peace process. In August, the Saudis felt they were close to persuading the PLO to give at least qualified recognition of United Nations Security Council Resolution 242 of November 22, 1966, calling for Israeli withdrawal of the occupied Arab territories. The Saudis believed that even qualified recognition of Resolution 242, with its implicit recognition of Israel's right to exist, would be sufficient to enable the United States to begin official talks with the PLO. PLO chairman Arafat had personally agreed to a formula developed by U.S. Secretary of State Cyrus Vance at Alexandria, which Egypt and the Saudis urged Arafat to accept. Under heavy Syrian pressure, however, the PLO Executive Committee demurred at the last moment, leaving the Saudis frustrated and embarrassed.[58]

Saudi optimism was further dashed on November 21, 1977, when President Sadat flew to Jerusalem. The Saudis saw their Arab diplomacy in ruins and Arab unity once again shattered. They were convinced that Sadat, having given up his one trump card—explicit recognition of the existence of Israel—had nothing left with which to negotiate a meaningful settlement with Israel.

The United States and other states counseled the Saudis to wait and see what resulted from Sadat's bold initiative, and the Saudis did not at first join in the general Arab criticism of the Sadat initiative. On the other hand, they ceased their attempts to forge an Arab consensus for negotiating a settlement.[59] By the summer of 1978, it appeared in Riyadh that, indeed, the Egyptian-Israeli peace talks would come to nothing. Because the Saudis were convinced that the most Sadat could obtain from Israel without U.S. pressure was a separate peace—that is, a return of Sinai for a separate Egyptian-Israeli peace treaty, but not resolution of the core issue of Palestinian rights of self-determination—the breakdown of the Sadat initiative did not particularly bother Riyadh. The Saudis saw a separate peace with Egypt as a play by Israel to split the Arab world and to deny to the Arabs Egyptian military support, potentially the only significant military threat to Israel.

Thus, when President Carter invited President Sadat and Prime Minister Begin to Camp David in September 1978, the Saudis did not appear to be overly apprehensive. They anticipated one of three possible outcomes: The United States would pressure Israel into making the requisite concessions on Palestinian rights to achieve a comprehensive settlement, a desirable but unlikely prospect; the United States would refrain from pressuring Israel but would state unequivocally its own position on Israeli withdrawal and Palestinian rights of self-determination, a lesser gain but slightly more likely; or, after appropriate, felicitous expressions of good intentions, the Sadat initiative would die a natural death, unlamented in the Arab world and proof to the entire world that Sadat's dramatic visit to Jerusalem was not sufficient to move Israel toward recognizing legitimate Palestinian rights, and hence toward peace.

None of these outcomes came to pass. The Camp David Accords, signed on September 17, 1978, were seen in Riyadh as the realization of their worst fears. Egypt was indeed making a separate peace with Israel, and the only provision for Palestinian self-determination was limited autonomy under Israeli control for the inhabitants of the West Bank and Gaza during a five-year transition period. No specific provisions were made for the Palestinian diaspora, including those refugees still in camps, and the whole question of the final disposition of the Occupied Arab Territories was to be put off until after the transition period.[60] The Saudis were additionally put out that an agreement so disadvantageous in their eyes had been concluded with no consultation with them or even with President Carter's personal envoy, Ambassador West.

U.S. and Egyptian assurances that the Camp David Accords were but the first step on a long road toward a final settlement were received with skepticism in Riyadh. The Saudis were convinced, particularly after Prime Minister Begin's strident remarks at the signing ceremonies about Jerusalem's being part of Israel, that Israel saw the accords as the penultimate step toward a settlement, lacking only cosmetic changes but no real concessions on Palestinian rights. Nevertheless, in large part at the urging of Ambassador West, the Saudis reserved final judgment.

The Carter administration wanted to believe that the Saudis supported the accords. Just before an Arab League summit to discuss Camp David in Baghdad in November 1978, the Saudis intimated that they would try to moderate the tone of the condemnations of the accords that were sure to be raised at the summit. To hopeful Washington, this was construed as passive support for the accords and even as a sign that the Saudis could be further counted upon to bring Jordan and the Palestinians (by whatever name) into the process.[61]

Although the Baghdad summit roundly condemned the accords, Carter, and Sadat, Saudi Crown Prince Fahd was able to prevent a complete Arab break with Egypt and claimed that the results would have been even worse without Saudi efforts at conciliation. This Fahd accomplished despite his "Three Member" Arab mission's to Cairo being rebuffed by Sadat. Nevertheless, the United States, led by its inflated expectations, was furious. President Carter felt personally betrayed by Crown Prince Fahd. Not only had the United States overestimated what the Saudis could do but what they would do. As Arabs no less opposed to the accords than their more immoderate fellow Arabs, the Saudis were never inclined directly to support the accords; and as participants in the Arab consensus, they were willing to moderate but not oppose the Arab condemnation of the Camp David Accords.[62]

The Saudi final judgment came when Egypt and Israel signed a peace treaty on March 26, 1979.[63] At the Arab League meeting convened in Baghdad in April to consider what actions to take against Egypt, Saudi Arabia supported the expulsion of Egypt from the league and the breaking of diplomatic and economic relations. It was not, however, willing to expel Egyptian workers from the Kingdom, sever airline service, or renege on prior aid commitments. From the point of view of U.S.-Saudi relations, the most important Saudi aid commitment was to fund most of a $525 million Egyptian purchase of fifty F-5Es. After a major speech by President Sadat on May 1, 1979, in which he launched a personal attack at the Saudi leadership, however, the Saudis withdrew the funding offer. Sadat's bold initiative had resulted in Egypt's becoming a pariah in the Arab world.

U.S.-Saudi relations were given an added strain with the departure of the shah from Iran on January 23, 1979, and the final collapse of the regime in February. With the United States in Saudi eyes unwilling or unable to save its close friend the shah, many leading Saudis wondered whether it would accord similar treatment to the Saudi regime in similar circumstances. Saudi confidence in U.S. intentions reached a new low. In an attempt to improve relations during this low point, the Carter administration invited Fahd to Washington. The timing of the visit coincided with the signing of the Egyptian-Israeli treaty in March, however, and Fahd canceled the visit, not wishing it to appear as implied support for the treaty.[64] The U.S.-Saudi "special relationship" was in disarray.

The Horn of Africa was another area where the Saudis entertained unrealistically high expectations of U.S. support. Somali President Siad Barre, who had come to power in 1969, developed close relations with the Soviet Union, which he allowed to build a naval base at Berbera. Siad was not only a self-styled socialist, but claimed all territories inhabited by Somali-speaking tribes, including the Ogaden, a huge arid area in neighboring Ethiopia. Although Siad had close ties with the Soviets, and Ethiopian Emperor Haile Selassie was pro-Western, the Saudis had a hard time supporting Ethiopia over Somalia. Haile Salassie was Christian and, in Saudi eyes, discriminated against Ethiopia's large Muslim population. Siad, on the other hand—despite his socialism—was still nominally a Muslim.

In September 1974, Haile Selassie was overthrown, and by 1977, Colonel Mengistu Haile Mariam had consolidated power by killing all his rivals. Mengistu was a Marxist and also established close relations with the Soviet Union. In 1977, the Soviets sided with Ethiopia over the Ogaden and facilitated Cuban military assistance to Mengistu to quell a Somali-instigated insurgency there. Deserted by the Soviets, Siad turned to the Arabs for help. To the Saudis, his position was much easier to support with the tables turned—Muslim Somalia against Marxist Ethiopia. Defense Minister Prince Sultan asked the United States and Britain to provide military assistance to Siad. Both countries temporized on grounds that the Somalis were clearly the aggressors in the Ogaden. The United States offered limited assistance to Siad but told him and the Saudis that full support was dependent on Siad's not pressing his claim to Ethiopian territory. Siad refused, and the Saudis were greatly frustrated at the unwillingness of the United States to counter what they saw as a clear Soviet-Cuban threat at the mouth of the Red Sea.[65]

Security and Diplomacy: In the 1980s

The fall of the shah was followed in December 1979 by the Soviet invasion of Afghanistan and in September 1980 by the outbreak of the Iran-Iraq war. South Yemen continued to foment revolution, and growing

Soviet influence in Marxist Ethiopia became another major security concern. Both the United States and Saudi Arabia became preoccupied with regional security issues, a preoccupation reflected in U.S.-Saudi political relations.

Faced with replacing the Two Pillar Policy, the Carter administration came up with its "Persian Gulf Strategy" and began to develop a rapid deployment force (RDF). In 1981, the incoming Reagan administration consciously downplayed the Arab-Israeli problem. On February 23, 1981, State Department spokesman William Dyes stated that the new administration would make its first priority in the Middle East the restoration of the West's strategic position against the Soviets. This task, he said, would take precedence over pressing ahead on Egyptian-Israeli negotiations on Palestinian autonomy.[66] The Reagan administration's focus on global security concerns led to the development of its "Strategic Consensus" policy for the area and—in the case of Saudi Arabia—to the sale of AWACS aircraft and the F-15 enhancement package (see Chapter 3).

The Fahd Plan

The renewed preoccupation with security issues once again emphasized to the Saudis the need for close cooperation with the United States. It did not, however, totally obscure political issues of mutual concern, nor did it incline the Saudis to accept U.S. dictates on policy formulation. Indeed, the Saudis were showing increasing signs of adjusting to their status as an oil power, and although they still felt strongly that it was vital to both countries to cooperate on mutual political and economic as well as security interests, they began to exercise a growing independence on how that cooperation should be accomplished. The first major Saudi initiative following the Sadat initiative occurred in mid-1981 with no prior consultation with the United States. On August 7, Crown Prince Fahd announced an eight-point plan for a comprehensive settlement of the Arab-Israeli problem. The points included

1. Israeli withdrawal from all Arab territory occupied in 1967, including East Jerusalem
2. The removal of Israeli settlements on Arab land established after 1967
3. Guaranteed freedom of worship for all religions in the Holy Places
4. Affirmation of the right of the Palestinian people to return to their homes and compensation to those who decide not to do so
5. UN control of the West Bank and Gaza Strip for a transitional period not exceeding a few months

6. The establishment of an independent Palestinian state with Jerusalem as its capital
7. Affirmation of the right of all states in the region to live in peace
8. The United Nations or some of its members to guarantee and implement these principles.[67]

The most controversial point was number seven, "affirmation of all states in the region to live in peace," which gave implicit recognition to the existence of Israel. Although Israel and its supporters later questioned this intention on grounds that the Saudis refused to address the recognition question more specifically or directly, it appears fairly certain that implied recognition was clearly the Saudi intention.

In presenting the plan, thereafter known as the Fahd Plan, Crown Prince Fahd had been careful to obtain prior consensus from the Arab states, including the PLO. According to some observers, Arafat had actually played a role in drafting the plan as a means for the PLO to play a role in the peace process independent from Syria. Arafat subsequently said that the plan could be the basis for working toward a lasting peace. In a separate statement, he welcomed the plan because it called for "coexistence" between the Arabs and Israel.[68]

Fahd himself said the plan was negotiable and that it was conceived as a "rational and balanced alternative" to the Camp David Accords, which had reached a dead end.[69] Although nothing in the Fahd Plan was specifically incompatible with the Camp David Accords (it was specific where the accords were general), and even though the Saudis said publicly that they did not expect Egypt to abrogate the accords, both Egypt and Israel objected to the Saudi proposal on the grounds that the accords constituted the only agreed-upon formula for seeking a settlement. Egyptian President Husni Mubarak intimated that it could be used as the basis of some future discussion, but Prime Minister Begin denounced it as an attempt "to liquidate Israel in stages"[70] and castigated Europe and the United States for cautious interest in the plan. In a letter to President Reagan on October 30, Begin condemned the entire plan and "warned" that any U.S. expressions of interest in it would be seen by the Arabs as a weakening of U.S. support for the Camp David Accords, making it more difficult for Israel and Egypt to agree on Palestinian autonomy.[71]

The United States was indeed caught in a ticklish position. The Saudis had obviously lost hope that the Americans would pressure Israel sufficiently to make requisite concessions for a settlement and had thus decided to pursue a peace initiative on their own. Moreover, there was an overall conciliatory tone to the Fahd Plan not matched by Israel's total rejection of it. Thus, while the Americans remained committed to the Camp David Accords, they did not want to discourage the Saudis altogether. On October 29, President Reagan said that the most significant aspect of the plan was that the Saudis recognized "Israel as a nation to be negotiated with." The same day, Secretary of State Alexander Haig noted that there were some aspects of the proposals "by which we are encouraged." On October 30, the State Department clearly reflected U.S. ambivalence, saying that while it welcomed some points, "certain other points in the plan [were] better left to negotiations."[72]

The Saudis announced their intention to propose the Fahd Plan for consideration at the Arab League summit, which was scheduled for November 25, 1981, in Fez, Morocco. They then set about winning Arab approval for the plan. Syria and Iraq, the two most formidable Arab hard-liners, were heavily in Saudi Arabia's debt, politically as well as financially. Iraq, in retreat in the Iran-Iraq war, was more dependent on Saudi Arabia. The Saudis had hoped this meant that Iraq and Syria could be persuaded not to oppose the plan, but at the presummit Arab foreign ministers' meeting on November 22, the two states finally came out against it. Syria pressured the PLO to do likewise. When the summit was convened three days later, King Hassan of Morocco, who was chairman, adjourned the meeting after four hours of discussion of the Fahd plan in order to avoid embarrassment for the Saudis.[73]

It is difficult to assess what impact the Fahd Plan would have had if it had been adopted by the Arab League. At the very least, the United States would have faced a serious dilemma. In contrast to the Camp David Accords, the Saudi proposal had broad Arab support and was not all that incompatible with previous U.S. policy positions on a settlement. On the other hand, the Israelis were unalterably opposed to it, holding fast to the Camp David Accords. Following the summit, Egyptian-Israeli talks on Palestinian autonomy continued, predictably getting nowhere. The Saudi attempt to break the impasse on Palestinian rights failed as had the Sadat initiative before it.

Aside from the Arab-Israeli problem, the events of 1979 and 1980 brought U.S.-Saudi political relations and U.S.-Saudi security concerns closer together. The trend had actually begun much earlier. The 1973-1974 energy crisis had transformed Saudi Arabia into a regional power and had persuaded the United States to enlist support and encourage Saudi diplomatic assistance for regional stability. This was particularly true in the case of the Lebanese Civil War, which broke out in 1975. Throughout the succeeding years, the Saudis established a special mediating role among the Lebanese factions, the PLO, and Syria that no other country, particularly the United States, could do. In fact, the Fahd Plan had reportedly taken shape during Saudi mediation efforts with the PLO to help bring about a cease-fire in the Lebanese situation in June 1981.[74]

The United States and Saudi Arabia also consulted over other security questions that involved them both, including the Polisario (Popular Front for the Liberation of Saquia-el-Hamra and Rio de Oro) insurgency in Morocco and support to the Afghans resisting the Soviet takeover of the country. Although the United States had no direct involvement in the Gulf Cooperation Council (GCC), it encouraged Saudi Arabia and other members to increase security cooperation in the face of threats from Iran, the Iran-Iraq war, and Soviet clients such as South Yemen. On the diplomatic side, Saudi Arabia achieved a rapprochement with Iraq, formerly a potential radical antagonist, and became a major financial supporter to that beleaguered state in its protracted war with Iran. By the end of 1983, even the United States had shifted its policy toward Iraq, informing the Gulf states that an Iraqi defeat in its war with Iran would be "contrary to U.S. interests."[75] At the same time, the Saudis also achieved at least a tactical rapprochement with its longtime antagonist, South Yemen.

The Reagan Plan and the Fez Proposal

The integration of security and diplomatic interests in U.S.-Saudi political relations was greatly accelerated on June 6, 1982, when Israeli armed forces invaded Lebanon with the intention of eliminating the PLO as a political and paramilitary force and of creating a friendly Maronite regime in Beirut. They did not fully accomplish either goal but did succeed in shattering the fragile cease-fire negotiated by the Americans with Saudi support in 1981. The invasion also shattered the tenuous balance of power among the Lebanese factions, leading to renewed and prolonged interconfessional hostilities.

The Saudis had long been involved diplomatically in Lebanon, but never had the stakes been so high. Following the Israeli invasion, even small successes or failures could mean the difference between renewed peace or renewed war. As the United States became more bogged down in Lebanon in 1983, and channels of communication with Syria became strained, Saudi diplomacy, despite its reduced chances of success, became more important. As with the peace process in general, greater Saudi involvement in Lebanon brought greater Saudi frustration against all the parties involved. Saudi ire at the PLO, Lebanese, and Syrians, however, did not neutralize frustration at the United States. It became particularly acute when, during Israeli Prime Minister Yitzak Shamir's visit to the United States in December 1983, U.S. policy shifted from efforts to play an evenhanded, mediator's role to one of confrontation with Syria and closer identification with Israel. The Saudi decision to turn to the French for a $4.5 billion purchase of air defense missiles, announced in January 1984, was at least in part a response to the perceived shift in U.S. policy toward Israel.[76]

Moreover, although the Saudis were frustrated at Syria's inflexibility over Lebanon, as well as over its support of Iran in the Iran-Iraq war, they continued to try to bring Assad back into the fold of Arab consensus and did not wish further to isolate him or to push Syria closer into the grasp of the Soviet Union. The Saudis were convinced that increased U.S. antagonism toward Syria and cooperation with Israel would do just that.

Such frustrations were probably inevitable once Saudi Arabia took for itself the role of moderate Arab mediator. It was, perhaps, a necessary role, but one that would continue to generate Saudi ambivalence in trying to maintain close political relations with the United States.

Israel's invasion of Lebanon did have the effect of inducing the United States, for the first time, to be more specific in its position on an overall Arab-Israeli settlement. In a major address on September 1, 1982, President Reagan stated that the United States had always sought to play the role of a mediator. "But it has become evident to me," he said, "that some clearer sense of America's position on key issues is necessary to encourage wider support for the peace process."[77] Reagan reaffirmed U.S. support for a five-year transition period outlined in the Camp David Accords, "during which the Palestinian inhabitants of the West Bank and Gaza will have full autonomy over their own affairs."[78] He added, "The United States will not support the use of any additional land for the purpose of settlements during the transition period. Indeed, the immediate adoption of a settlement freeze by Israel, more than any other action, could create the confidence needed for wider participation in these talks."[79]

Looking toward a final settlement, President Reagan said that the United States would support neither Israeli annexation or permanent control of the West Bank and Gaza nor a Palestinian state. "But it is the firm view of the United States that self-government by the Palestinians of the West Bank and Gaza in association with Jordan offers the best chance for a durable, just and lasting peace."[80] Reagan also called for an undivided Jerusalem, the status of which should be determined by negotiation. The Reagan plan, as it was called, was immediately rejected by Israeli Prime Minister Begin. On September 5, the Israeli Cabinet allocated funds for three new settlements and approved seven more. On September 8, the Knesset (Israel's parliament) rejected the Reagan Plan by a vote of fifty to thirty-six.[81]

Arab reaction was much more positive. At the Arab League summit meeting in Fez, Morocco, September 5–8, an eight-point counterproposal was adopted:

1. Israeli withdrawal from all occupied Arab territories including East Jerusalem
2. Dismantling of Israeli settlements in the Arab territories
3. Guarantees for freedom of worship for all religious and rites
4. Affirmation of Palestinian rights of self-determination and exercise of those rights under their sole representative, the PLO
5. A transition period of a few months for the West Bank and Gaza supervised by the United Nations
6. Establishment of a Palestinian state with Jerusalem its capital
7. Guarantee of the peace and security of all states in the region, including a Palestinian state, by the United Nations Security Council
8. Guarantee of the implementation of these principles by the Security Council.[82]

The 1982 Fez proposal bore a striking resemblance to the Fahd Plan.[83] Though not so forthcoming as the original Fahd Plan, it had the merit of Arab League consensus, contained an indirect recognition of the existence of Israel (in point seven), and was not totally incompatible with the Camp David Accords, at least as a negotiating position. Thus, even though the Saudi's proposal failed in 1981, they saw their efforts bear fruit a year later. Unfortunately, by that time the Lebanese crisis had so occupied Middle East security and politics that little attention could be given to the peace process. In early 1984, the United States withdrew from Lebanon, and international and regional focus on that problem diminished considerably. The Reagan Plan and the Fez proposal still remain on the table as points of departure for future U.S.-Arab dialogue on a peace settlement. In any such dialogue, Saudi Arabia is bound to play a major role.

Notes

1. U.S. Department of State, *Foreign Relations of the United States,* vol. 2 (Washington, D.C.: Government Printing Office, 1931), pp. 547–554 (hereinafter cited as *FRUS* with volume and year).

2. Aaron David Miller, *Search for Security: Saudi Arabian Oil and American Foreign Policy, 1939–1949* (Chapel Hill: University of North Carolina Press, 1980), p. 25.

3. The agreement was signed in London by the U.S. ambassador and the Saudi minister to the United Kingdom. *FRUS,* vol. 2, 1933, pp. 995–1001.

4. Miller, *Search for Security,* p. 25.

5. Ibid.

6. Ibid., p. 228, n. 101.

7. Ibid., p. 237, n. 80; and Malcolm Peck, "Saudi Arabia in United States Foreign Policy to 1958: A Case Study in the Sources and Determinants of American Policy" (Ph.D. dissertation, Fletcher School of Law and Diplomacy, 1970), p. 156.

8. For a summary of the mission's report, issued in March 1943, see United Kingdom, Geographical Handbook Series, *Western Arabia and the Red Sea,* June 1946, pp. 474–475. See also *FRUS,* vol. 4, 1942, p. 564.

9. Peck, "Saudi Arabia in United States Foreign Policy," p. 153.

10. Ibid., p. 157.

11. Memorandum from Jesse Jones, Federal Loan Agency administrator, to the secretary of state, *FRUS,* vol. 3, 1941, p. 646.

12. *FRUS,* vol. 4, 1942, p. 569.

13. *FRUS,* vol. 4, 1943, p. 871.

14. George Kirk, *The Middle East in the War* (New York and London: Oxford University Press, 1953), p. 367, n. 2; George A. Brownell, "American Aviation in the Middle East," *Middle East Journal* 1, no. 9 (1947), p. 409. For a discussion of the Dhahran air base, see Chapter 3.

15. Miller discusses in detail the fears of the State Department's Near East Division and the oil companies of British intentions toward Saudi oil. See Miller, *Search for Security,* chap. 3, "Crude Diplomacy: The United States and Arabian Oil, 1943," especially pp. 64–71.

16. Peck, "Saudi Arabia in United States Foreign Policy," p. 158.

17. Ibid.

18. Robert Lacey, *The Kingdom* (London: Hutchinson, 1981) p. 265.

19. Miller, *Search for Security,* p. 109.

20. Ibid.

21. Lacey, *The Kingdom,* p. 266.

22. See William A. Eddy, *FDR Meets Ibn Saud* (New York: American Friends of the Middle East, 1954).

23. Peck, "Saudi Arabia in United States Foreign Policy," pp. 176–177.

24. *FRUS,* vol. 4, 1943, pp. 796–797, 808–812.

25. Peck, "Saudi Arabia in United States Foreign Policy," p. 180.

26. *Congressional Record,* 79th Cong., 1st sess., vol. 91, pt. 2 (1945), p. 1622.

27. Peck, "Saudi Arabia in United States Foreign Policy," p. 180. The letter was quoted in Edward R. Stettinius, Jr., *Roosevelt and the Russians,* edited by Walter Johnson (New York: Doubleday and Company, 1949), pp. 289–290.

28. Eddy, *FDR Meets Ibn Saud,* p. 37.

29. Peck, "Saudi Arabia in United States Foreign Policy," p. 202. According to Ambassador Hermann Eilts, Faysal was particularly bitter at Secretary of

State George Marshall over the UN vote, though Marshall was only carrying out instructions. Personal communication, June 11, 1984.

30. Department of State *Bulletin,* November 10, 1946, pp. 848–850.

31. Peck, "Saudi Arabia in United States Foreign Policy," p. 200. Ambassador Hermann Eilts recounted to me an amusing account of Child's presenting his letters of credence to the king at the old Murubba palace in Riyadh. Childs, unaccustomed to the long white thaub all were required to wear at a royal audience, tripped on the mud brick floor as he backed out of the royal presence. His entire staff of junior officers, Eilts and Donald Bergus, not seeing him go down, thereupon tripped over him and also went down. The only reaction of King Abd al-Aziz, whose eyesight was failing him, to the American Embassy on its posteriors was to keep shouting "*Aysh hadha* (What is that)?"

32. *New York Times,* March 28, 1954, p. 1, quoted in Peck, "Saudi Arabia in United States Foreign Policy," p. 248.

33. Ibid.

34. Robert H. Ferrell, ed., *The Eisenhower Diaries* (New York and London: W. W. Norton, 1981), p. 319.

35. See also J. B. Kelly, *Arabia, the Gulf and the West* (New York: Basic Books, 1980), p. 60.

36. See Saudi Arabia, *Memorial of the Government of Saudi Arabia: Arbitration for the Settlement of the Territorial Dispute Between Muscat and Abu Dhabi on the One Side and Saudi Arabia on the Other,* A.H. 1374/A.D. 1955; and United Kingdom, Parliamentary Debates, *Arbitration Concerning Buryaimi and the Common Frontier Between Abu Dhabi and Sa'udi Arabia: Memorial Submitted by the Government of the United Kingdom of Great Britain and Northern Ireland,* 1955.

37. I was then a political analyst for the Arabian Peninsula at the State Department and drafted a small report on the resolution of this historic dispute. The report, however, was never published due to its lack of any "policy relevance."

38. The Suez crisis is well documented. One of the more objective brief accounts is found in Fred J. Khouri, *The Arab-Israeli Dilemma,* 2d ed. (Syracuse, N.Y.: Syracuse University Press, 1976), pp. 210–219.

39. John C. Campbell, *Defense of the Middle East,* rev. ed. (New York: Frederick A. Praeger, 1960), p. 122.

40. Ibid., pp. 264–265. Many of the congressional epithets hurled at the Saudis over the debate bear a certain resemblance to those used over two decades later in the F-15 and AWACS debates, lending a certain aura of *déjà vu* to the records of those events.

41. Ibid., p. 263.

42. U.S. Congress, House of Representatives, *Economic and Military Cooperation with Nations in the Middle East,* hearings before the Committee on Foreign Affairs on H.J. Res. 117 (Eisenhower Doctrine), 85th Cong., 1st sess. (Washington, D.C.: Government Printing Office, 1957), pp. 7–8, 26.

43. U.S. Congress, Senate, *The President's Proposal on the Middle East* (Eisenhower Doctrine), hearings before the Committee on Foreign Relations and the Committee on Armed Services on S.J. Res. and H.J. Res. 117, pt. 2 (Washington, D.C.: Government Printing Office, 1957), p. 665.

44. Peck, "Saudi Arabia in United States Foreign Policy," p. 266.

45. Personal communication from Ambassador Hermann Eilts, June 11, 1984.

46. For a discussion of the Ten Point Reform Program, see David Holden and Richard Johns, *The House of Saud* (London: Sidgwick and Jackson, 1981), pp. 229–231; and Lacey, *The Kingdom,* pp. 344–345.

47. Holden and Johns, *The House of Saud,* p. 233.

48. Ibid. Faysal, in response to a periodic U.S. *démarche* for reform during this period, once replied to Ambassador Eilts, "Do you think I want Saudi Arabia to become like the Berkeley campus?" Personal communication, June 11, 1984.

49. For accounts of the 1969 al-Wadiy'ah incident, see Holden and Johns, *The House of Saud,* pp. 281–282; and Anthony H. Cordesman, *The Gulf and the Search for Strategic Stability* (Boulder, Colo.: Westview Press; and London: Mansell Publishing; 1984), p. 139.

50. Cited in Holden and Johns, *The House of Saud,* p. 357.

51. William B. Quandt, *Saudi Arabia's Oil Policy* (Washington, D.C.: Brookings Institution, 1982), p. 50.

52. Ibid.

53. Department of State *Bulletin,* November 4, 1974, p. 612.

54. Ibid.

55. *Middle East Journal,* 31, no. 1 (Winter 1977), p. 57.

56. Richard M. Preece, "The Saudi Peace Proposals" (Washington, D.C.: Congressional Research Service, the Library of Congress, November 24, 1981), p. 4.

57. Ibid.

58. Quandt, *Saudi Arabia's Oil Policy,* p. 113.

59. During President Carter's visit to Riyadh in January 1978, the Saudis did agree to a formula supporting the right of the Palestinians "to participate in the determination of their own future." Later known as the Aswan formula, it was incorporated in the Camp David Accords. Quandt, *Saudi Arabia's Oil Policy,* p. 144, n. 4.

60. For the text of the Camp David Accords, see U.S. Department of State, *American Foreign Policy: Basic Documents, 1977–1980* (Washington, D.C.: Government Printing Office, 1983), documents 290–294, pp. 652–662.

61. Quandt, *Saudi Arabia's Oil Policy,* p. 114.

62. Ibid.

63. U.S. Department of State, *American Foreign Policy,* document 302, pp. 669–683.

64. Quandt, *Saudi Arabia's Oil Policy,* p. 115.

65. Holden and Johns, *The House of Saud,* pp. 469–474.

66. Department of State, press briefing, February 23, 1981.

67. Preece, "The Saudi Peace Proposals," p. 2.

68. Ibid., p. 7.

69. Ibid., p. 3.

70. Ibid., p. 5.

71. Ibid., pp. 9–10.

72. Ibid., p. 9.
73. *Middle East Journal* 36, no. 2 (Spring 1982), p. 222.
74. Preece, "The Saudi Peace Proposals," p. 3.
75. *Washington Post,* January 1, 1984, p. A1.
76. *Time,* December 12, 1983, p. 19; *New York Times,* January 17, 1984, p. A1; *Washington Post,* January 17, 1984, p. A1.
77. U.S. Department of State, *The Quest for Peace: Principal United States Statements and Documents Relating to the Arab-Israeli Peace Process, 1967–1983* (Washington, D.C.: Government Printing Office, 1983), p. 107.
78. Ibid.
79. Ibid., p. 108.
80. Ibid.
81. *Middle East Journal* 37, no. 1 (Winter 1983), p. 71.
82. Ibid.
83. One Washington wag dubbed it "Son-of-Fahd Plan."

6
Ambivalent Allies

Tracing U.S.-Saudi relations to their historical origins has revealed the singular degree of continuity that has characterized the relationship. This stable community of interests has further been characterized by the relatively independent sets of dynamics that have guided each of its four major components—oil, military security, economic and commercial concerns, and politics.[1]

Generally, both the Saudis and the Americans have attempted to keep these component sets of relations separate, but for the most part they have failed. Linkages among them have always existed. In times of crisis, these linkages have tended to become more pronounced, particularly the negative linkages. The so-called oil weapon used by the Saudis against the United States in 1973, for example, linked oil and politics; the at-times acrimonious U.S. congressional debates over the sale of F-15 and AWACS aircraft to Saudi Arabia linked military cooperation and politics; and the Arab oil embargo and U.S. antiboycott, tax, and trade legislation linked politics and economics.

A second characteristic of U.S.-Saudi relations has been the constant undercurrent of ambivalence that has permeated the relationship as a whole and each of its component parts. Anomalies exist in every aspect of U.S.-Saudi relations. The differences between the two countries over the Arab-Israeli problem, the differences inherent in the United States' being the world's leading oil consumer and Saudi Arabia's being the world's leading oil-exporting country, the predominantly global focus of the United States and the predominantly regional focus of Saudi Arabia, and the secular political orientation of the United States in contrast to the religious political orientation of Saudi Arabia are but a few of the underlying sources of ambivalence.

On balance, U.S. and Saudi mutual interests outweigh mutual antagonisms, a basic factor in the longevity and resilience of the relationship. Ambivalence, however, does place a constraint on the degree of cooperation possible within the relationship, and it would be naive to assume that ambivalence can be removed entirely. Failure to recognize this fact has led all too often in the past to unrealistic expectations of what one side is willing, able, or likely to do in support of the other's interests.

Perhaps the greatest irony of all is how two peoples with such total cultural disparity—more so than between the United States and virtually any other Arab state—have been able to get along for so long as well as they have. There are bridges, to be sure: The Saudis place high store in the United States as a God-fearing nation, and the Americans place high store in Saudi Arabia's strident anticommunism. But notwithstanding the two countries' long association, the many Saudis who have been educated in the United States, and the growing numbers of Americans who have lived and worked in Saudi Arabia, the two peoples remain very foreign to each other. Very few westerners really understand the Saudi mentality, and very few Saudis become as Western in thought as they do in manner.

The answer to why the relationship has weathered so well appears to be that—despite misunderstandings, unrealistic expectations, and divergent policies by each side—each country has benefited greatly from the other's friendship. Moreover, the ambivalence that permeates the relationship has created a tension such that neither side can any longer quite take the other for granted. In a world of competing interests, this is not altogether a bad thing.

A Continuity of Independent Interests

Oil and regional security interests togther have provided the major threads of continuity in U.S.-Saudi relations from the beginning. For the most part, the U.S. government has maintained a noninterventionist policy on oil relations, allowing the private sector and market forces to determine price and production rates. Major exceptions to this tendency occurred in the 1940s and 1970s. In the first instance, the United States, concerned about the availability of oil, negotiated for a time to buy equity in Aramco. The second instance took place when the transfer of price- and production-setting authority from the oil companies to OPEC members forced the United States to create a government-to-government relationship with Saudi Arabia and other key OPEC members on the question of oil. Although these government-to-government relations are still a vital and integral part of U.S. energy policy, the oil glut of the 1980s has again reinforced the primacy of market forces over direct government intervention in U.S.-Saudi oil relations.

Saudi oil interests have evolved in a somewhat different direction. Prior to the 1970s, the oil companies rather than the oil-producing countries more or less dictated oil price and production levels. The

Iranian experience with the nationalization of their oil resources under Mossadeq in the early 1950s was a grim reminder to any oil-producing country of the risks of trying to seize control of the assets owned by the oil companies under concession agreements. At the same time, revenues were a mutual concern of both Saudi Arabia and Aramco, and increasing production was for both a greater priority than conservation. With these priorities shared by other oil producers and companies, production increased and real prices remained low until demand finally outstripped available supply. In 1970, the United States became a net oil importer, and soon thereafter the energy crisis ushered in a new order in the international oil market. With the resulting transfer of both equity and control over oil production from the oil companies to the oil-producing countries, the latter, including Saudi Arabia, began to direct upstream oil operations as a matter of government policy, a situation that still exists.

Since then, Saudi oil policy has reflected the Kingdom's interest in higher oil prices, but it has also reflected its interest in maintaining market stability. Precipitate price increases and declines have been no more welcome to Saudi Arabia than they were to the oil companies when they controlled prices. Albeit with less success than the companies formerly had, Saudi Arabia has been a leader in seeking market stability. Within OPEC, the Saudis have more or less consistently tried to use their position as the world's key oil exporter to be the swing producer, moderating both upward and downward pressures on prices. For example, in 1977, Saudi Arabia was joined by the UAE in breaking ranks with other OPEC producers to raise prices by only 5 percent rather than 10 percent. In mid-1977 they raised prices another 5 percent to restore price unity but only in return for a price freeze that would allow inflation to lower real prices. To strengthen their position, the Saudis kept production high during 1977 to soften the market.[2]

In October 1980, the Saudis again increased production in response to the outbreak of the Iran-Iraq war, fearing another precipitate price hike.[3] In 1981, they maintained high production rates and again broke ranks with OPEC, keeping their oil at $32.00 per barrel while the price hawks insisted on $36.40.[4] By 1982, however, the situation was reversed as the oil market entered a period of glut. Saudi Arabia then began cutting production to prevent prices from declining. Although they were not wholly successful (OPEC posted prices dropped to $29.00 per barrel in March 1983), their effort did have a braking effect on the rate of decline.

On balance, Saudi Arabia, as the leading OPEC producer, has played a much more interventionist role in oil matters than has the United States. In both cases, however, world market conditions—as much as if not more so than political or other factors relating to Saudi oil policy—have continued to play the predominant role in determining prices and production rates. A mutual interest in stable market conditions, therefore, has provided the grounds for cooperation in oil matters despite the divergence in buyer-seller interests.

Security concerns have been at the heart of U.S.-Saudi relations since the Kingdom was first granted Lend-Lease eligibility during World War II. Over the years, the nature of security needs has changed, but the centrality of security and military concerns to the overall relationship remains constant. World War II was followed by the cold war of the 1950s, the Nasserist threat of the 1960s, a reemergence of the Soviet threat in the late 1970s coupled with the threat to Gulf stability of revolutionary Iran, and, in 1980, the Iran-Iraq war.

Over the years, close U.S.-Saudi military relations have evolved, with the United States serving as the principal military advisor to the Kingdom. Following the energy crisis of 1973-1974, the Saudis decided to accelerate their military development programs and had money to do so. Most of the spending went into military construction, but large Saudi military purchases from the United States began to draw U.S. congressional criticism. This situation led to a series of crises of Saudi confidence in the U.S. commitment to the security of the Kingdom, particularly following the downfall of the shah of Iran in 1979. Moreover, Saudi arms requests were by and large based on U.S. surveys and recommendations. By the late 1970s, the Saudis began to view U.S. responses to arms requests as "litmus tests" of friendship. The fight for congressional approval of F-15s and AWACS, against strong pro-Israeli opposition, thus took on a psychological as well as a political dimension.

Nevertheless, U.S.-Saudi relations survived these strains intact. Although the Arab-Israeli problem does impede cooperation over such issues as use of military installations and prepositioning of matériel for times of crisis, cooperation to deter possible military threats in the Gulf has been possible. In particular, the security threat created by the ongoing Iran-Iraq war has remained an impetus for continued close U.S.-Saudi cooperation on security matters.

To a great degree, economic and commercial relations have also developed patterns independently of other areas of interest, albeit they stem almost entirely from Saudi Arabia's huge oil resources. Both the United States and Saudi Arabia recognize the need for massive Saudi foreign-currency holdings to be managed in a way that will not threaten the international monetary system. The Saudis, with their huge wealth invested mainly in the major money markets of the West, are acutely aware that their own economic well-being depends on the well-being of the free world economy. On the commercial side, Saudi Arabia needs goods, services, and technology transfers that the United States can provide and has a special appreciation for U.S. technology and business practices. For its part, the United States needs export markets.

Commercial relations have generally been free of government interference by either country. Exceptions have been Saudi adherence to the Arab boycott and U.S. self-inflicted restrictions of trade through foreign tax, commercial practices, and antiboycott legislation. Although this legislation has become much less restrictive since the late 1970s, it has contributed to the loss of thousands of U.S. jobs and millions of dollars in U.S. exports to Saudi Arabia alone. These exceptions, however, have not seriously undermined the close U.S.-Saudi commercial relations that began with the first oil men to walk ashore at the then small village of Jubayl in the early 1930s.

U.S.-Saudi political relations lagged behind oil and military relations until the 1970s. With the emergence of Saudi Arabia as a major leader of the Arab moderates after 1973, the United States began to consider Saudi support of the Arab-Israeli peace process to be crucial. Neither country has envisioned or desired the Kingdom as an actual party to peace negotiations, but the United States has actively sought both behind-the-scenes efforts and public Saudi support for the peace process. The United States was therefore greatly disappointed that the Saudis declined to support the Camp David Accords and the subsequent Israeli-Egyptian peace treaty, which, with all its shortcomings, was viewed in Washington as the best available vehicle for achieving an Arab-Israeli settlement. Nevertheless, the United States has continued to look to Saudi Arabia to play a leading moderating and stabilizing role in the Arab world and a strong supportive role in the Arab-Israeli peace process, including efforts in the 1982–1984 period to effect a withdrawal of foreign forces from Lebanon.

The Saudis, possibly even more than the Americans, have viewed the Arab-Israeli problem as the greatest threat to regional stability. So long as the problem remains, the Saudis believe that it will factionalize and radicalize the Arab world, make dealings with the United States difficult, and maximize opportunities for Soviet expansion in the area. In Saudi eyes, the sine qua non for a settlement is recognition of Palestinian rights of self-determination. The Saudis' opposition to the Camp David process was based on the conviction that it provided no avenue for the realization of full Palestinian rights. That done, they believe that they and the other Arab moderates could deliver the Arab side on other contentious issues.

Realistically, the Saudis do not have much hope that the United States has the will to coerce Israel toward accepting Palestinian rights, at least in the near term. Nevertheless, they believe that their task must continue to be to encourage the United States toward that necessary step. In the meantime, as a leader of the Arab moderates, Saudi Arabia believes it must seek to avoid Arab intransigence toward a negotiated settlement against that time when real progress toward peace is possible.

Linkages Among Interests

The independent nature of oil, military, political, and economic-commercial relations does not mean that the links among them are unimportant. The Arab oil embargo, engineered mainly by Saudi Arabia, must certainly dispel that idea. In retrospect, however, the embargo was not oil policy at all but a political policy using oil as its instrument for implementation. Moreover, punitive oil policies are not the usual Saudi style. It has been far more the case that where oil and politics are linked negatively, the Saudis have chosen to be less accommodating rather than outright punitive, preferring to sit on their hands.

There is probably a greater linkage between oil and politics in the more positive context of seeking to expand U.S. cooperation in the areas of interest to the Kingdom. The Saudis are certainly aware that the United States acts not simply from friendship but out of self-interest and assume that the same is true about U.S. awareness of Saudi motives. It has therefore been the tendency by Saudi Arabia, in accommodating the United States and the West, to go incrementally beyond what its narrow oil interests might dictate in moderating oil prices as an attempt to create an atmosphere of mutual trust and cooperation in pursuit of Saudi political interests. This is particularly so in Saudi desires to encourage the United States to be more forceful with Israel in the Arab-Israeli peace process on the subject of Palestinian rights of self-determination in the occupied Arab territories.

The linkage between oil and security has been even closer. As Saudi Arabia has risen to become the free world's leading oil exporter, U.S. concern for securing the flow of Saudi oil has increased—over questions ranging from oil-field security to regional political security. This linkage has provided a mutuality of interests in military and security cooperation that has enabled U.S.-Saudi military relations to develop a long-term continuity and a dynamic that has transcended specific issues and crises that have confronted the relationship over the years.

On the Saudi side, the discovery of oil brought to an end the formerly endemic financial insecurity that had plagued the region, but it also created a new anxiety over political security for a country of vast oil resources and only the most rudimentary armed and security forces with which to defend itself. The Saudis have viewed the United States not only as the world's principal energy consumer but also as the political and military leader of the free world. From this perspective, Saudi Arabia has considered the linkage of oil and security in U.S.-Saudi relations as a partnership in which Saudi Arabia would endeavor to secure oil flows to the West and the United States would provide military security—directly if required, but preferably indirectly through military assistance—to Saudi Arabia and other friendly Gulf states.

The United States and Saudi Arabia also share a common perception of the Soviet Union as the primary threat to regional security. The Soviet threat is both direct, as in Afghanistan and Ethiopia, and indirect, through military and intelligence support of regimes friendly to the Soviet Union and through support for subversive and dissident groups and movements. Thus military security, regional security, and internal political stability are also closely linked.

There are other linkages between oil and security relations and economic-commercial relations. Not only is the Saudi economy based on oil, but the economic well-being of the United States is linked inexorably with the price of oil. A more important link, particularly in the Saudi view, is that between a strong Western economy and the will and ability of the West to withstand the threat of Soviet political and military expansion. This concern is accordingly reflected in Saudi international economic and monetary policies.

Saudi commercial activity and hence U.S. commercial opportunities are obviously tied to Saudi oil income, but also to security considerations. Military sales have constituted one of the largest increments of total U.S. exports to Saudi Arabia. The United States first realized the purely commercial aspects of military sales to Saudi Arabia in the 1960s with the implementation of major new Saudi military development plans. Whereas commercial gain was never so paramount in Washington's military sales policies as it was with some other military suppliers, the economic advantages of military sales could no longer be ignored.

Linkages among and between areas of major interest are more visible at some times than at others. They are most obvious during crisis situations such as the Arab oil embargo (oil and politics) or during periods of high political interest, such as during the seeking of U.S. congressional approval for the sale of F-15s and AWACS aircraft to Saudi Arabia (military and political interests). Far less obvious are the nature and extent of ongoing, long-term linkages. Generally speaking, such linkages are neither so sinister as they are labeled by many political analysts nor compelling enough to appreciably undermine the independent dynamics of each separate area of interest. It would be ridiculous, for example, to assume that the oil weapon is a constant major component of Saudi energy policy or that often highly publicized Saudi arms requests are based more on immediate political concerns than on long-term development planning, generally provided by the United States.

An Undercurrent of Ambivalence

The United States and Saudi Arabia have both maintained a degree of ambivalence toward their mutual relations from the very beginning. The issues over which they have equivocated have changed somewhat over the years, but the underlying roots of ambivalence have remained remarkably stable.

For the United States, the roots of ambivalence have centered on its great power status and—after World War II—on its superpower status. As such, it has many competing and often conflicting interests, not only in the Middle East but globally. A large part of U.S. diplomacy, therefore, has of necessity focused on attempts to accommodate these competing interests through trade-offs, compromises, and equivocal policies. U.S. ambivalence toward Saudi Arabia has centered to a large degree on concern not to give the Kingdom a blank check that could possibly involve the United States in commitments beyond the scope of the relationship. After the creation of Israel in 1948, the Arab-Israeli problem has been a major focus of U.S. ambivalence, as Washington has sought to avoid conflicts between its commitments with Israel and those with Saudi Arabia.

A related element has been a difference in U.S. and Saudi perceptions of mutual security. Both sides have long viewed the Soviet Union and its radical allies in the region as the primary threat to regional stability and to Saudi internal security. The United States has therefore been much less equivocal than Saudi Arabia in its efforts to oppose Arab radicalism and has tended to interpret Saudi reluctance to take punitive actions against the Arab radicals as a result of their intimidation of the Saudi regime. The interpretation, although valid to a degree, does not fully take into account the fact that Saudi Arabia is itself an Arab state. It strongly and sincerely espouses the Arab cause—self-determination for the Palestinians—and also espouses—to the extent possible—freedom of the entire region from global politics in which superpower interests rather than regional interests are paramount.

Another area of U.S. ambivalence toward Saudi Arabia is oil. With the United States a major importer and Saudi Arabia a major exporter, a certain degree of ambivalence is inevitable. To the extent, for instance, that Saudi pricing policies do not match U.S. interests, a broader dialogue is necessary that could, as one example, make political or security assistance a trade-off for price concessions. For such a dialogue to be successful, however, each side must have a very clear idea of the other's priorities as well as its own. One anomaly in U.S.-Saudi oil relations is more apparent than real. In the early 1970s, the United States imported very little Saudi oil. The amount rose dramatically in the 1970s and has since declined sharply in the oil glut of the 1980s, leading some Americans to believe they need no longer worry about Saudi oil policies. The fact is that the United States cannot insure oil security by diversifying its sources of supply. What counts is aggregate supply-demand relationships, not patterns of trade. A glut or a shortage will affect the entire market no matter what those patterns are.

Saudi ambivalence is to a great degree complementary to U.S. ambivalence. It has centered on the concerns of a small power seeking a balanced relationship with a superpower. The disparity of power has produced anxiety among Saudi leaders that they could become suffocated in the embrace of their U.S. friends. Saudis are intensely proud of their independence and extremely anxious to avoid any suggestion of a diminution of sovereignty. Thus no matter how strong U.S.-Saudi mutual interests have been, the Saudis have consistently endeavored to maintain a degree of distance between themselves and the United States commensurate with their desire to maintain independence of action.

The Arab-Israeli problem has also been a primary focus of Saudi ambivalence toward the United States. While sharing the U.S. view that communism and Arab radicalism have constituted the greatest long-term strategic threats to Saudi and regional security, the Saudis believe that the Arab-Israeli problem is the greater immediate threat. Since they also believe that the United States, as the vital supporter of Israel, has the primary responsibility for impelling Israel to accept the validity of Palestinian aspirations, they see lack of progress toward a settlement as largely the fault of the United States and as a major impediment toward less equivocal cooperation in mutual interests in other areas, notably in military cooperation.

By the late 1970s, a new source of ambivalence appeared on the scene: Islamic fundamentalism. Prior to that time, conventional wisdom had been that the younger generation in Muslim societies, if their aggregate political, economic, and social expectations were sufficiently frustrated, would turn to radical political ideologies as a means of expressing their disaffection with the status quo. Certainly many young Muslims will continue to seek meaning to their ever more confusing lives through radical socialist and nationalist doctrines, but these doctrines no longer can be considered the only avenue open to the disaffected. Moreover, given commonly perceived antagonists (for example, Western colonialism, imperialism, and capitalism), militant radical and Islamic movements can, at least temporarily, enter a symbiotic relationship that has sometimes been described as Islamic socialism.

Militant Islamic revival movements have been on the scene for centuries. Saudi Arabia's own Wahhabi revival is nearly 250 years old. Even the contemporary Muslim Brotherhood, founded in Egypt by Hassan al-Banna, is over 60 years old. The popular appeal of these movements, however, was relatively limited, whereas the current resurgence of Islamic fundamentalism is widespread. On the other hand, it does not appear to be a monolithic political movement, and few generalizations can be made about the phenomenon as a whole. Its appeal seems to be more negative than positive and more sociological than theological, stemming from the growing inability to cope with the social disorientation created by rapid modernization since World War II. (As such, it is not far removed from Christian, Jewish, Hindu, and even Sikh fundamentalist movements.) The new Muslim fundamentalists also share a fanatic intolerance for all who do not totally agree with them. For the most part, neither the United States nor Saudi Arabia has been spared the enmity of the most militant fundamentalists, notably the Iranians.

For Saudi Arabia, the new fundamentalism is particularly perplexing. It does not fit the Saudi world view of monotheism in confrontation with secular atheism upon which most of Saudi foreign policy is based. Even worse, it challenges the Saudi regime's own claim to political legitimacy through the conservative Islamic orthodoxy of the Wahhabi revival. It is a threat from the right for a country that has seen itself as the spokesman for the right and that has traditionally confronted threats from the left. The challenge is even more serious in its rejection of the modernization and economic development efforts the Saudis have so assiduously pursued over the past forty years.

The United States has been no less perplexed than Saudi Arabia at how to react to the new Islamic fundamentalism. It equally does not conform to U.S. notions of a bipolar world. Although stridently anti-Western, Muslim fundamentalists are no less anti-Communist, and it is difficult for Americans to grapple with a major threat to their interests from an anti-Communist source. For example, many are still seeking to construct a thesis whereby, no matter what happens in Iran, it will almost inevitably redound to Soviet advantage, despite the fact that the Iran-Iraq war has placed the Soviets in a dilemma by which their support of Iraq threatens their close relations with Syria and their desire not to antagonize Iran.[5]

U.S. and Saudi ambivalence on how to deal with the new Islamic fundamentalism is therefore as much over the phenomenon itself as over its impact on U.S.-Saudi relations. Saudi Arabia seeks U.S. assistance in defending itself against internal and external security threats posed by Muslim fundamentalists, but at the same time recognizes that overly close U.S. ties are a potential rallying cry for religious zealots seeking to rid the region of all vestiges of Westernization. The United States also realizes the limits on its ability to assist the Saudis and is thus chary of rendering assistance that could be counterproductive. Moreover, the United States is virtually powerless to respond in cases of indigenous internal insecurity. Islamic fundamentalism is an area in which both countries will probably continue to feel their way cautiously for the foreseeable future.

Balancing the Interests

Because of the preponderance of mutual interests over mutual antagonisms, the realization of U.S. and Saudi policy goals can better be obtained through cooperation rather than confrontation. One of the problems for the United States in entering cooperative relationships with a weaker state is that such an arrangement severely limits the use of superior power in pursuit of policy goals. Such superiority is mainly effective in a confrontational relationship. Thus, such lines of reasoning as "they need us more than we need them" are self-defeating. If the United States truly believes that its needs are best served through cooperation with Saudi Arabia, then a calculation of the preponderance of the need should not be a consideration. Instead, the terms of the relationship should be determined on the basis of which side can do more to meet the other's needs—in other words, not by which side needs the most, but by which side can contribute the most. The Saudis do not mind so much acknowledging their need for U.S. cooperation. For them, the problem is what they perceive to be a U.S. unwillingness to acknowledge that it needs Saudi cooperation as well.

With the preponderance of power and influence, the United States should not have insurmountable difficulty in establishing an acceptable quid pro quo for cooperation with the Saudis. For example, if a U.S.-dictated Arab-Israeli settlement and U.S. military base rights in Saudi Arabia are both out of the question, it should still not be impossible to work out a quid pro quo of something less than a settlement in return for something less than base rights. The important thing is to accept the essentially cooperative nature of the relationship and the constraints on each side to meet the other's expectations.

A final word should be said about the value of personal diplomacy. Security is in many ways a psychological factor. It is true that one can, to a degree, quantify military capability, but it is more difficult to quantify the degree of deterrence that capability will produce and hence how much security it can bring. Saudi Arabia, because of its unique history and its current status as the world's key oil exporter lacking the military means to defend itself, is preoccupied with security as few other small states are. The periodic reassurance of support for the security of the regime that the Saudis wish from the United States is therefore highly psychological in nature.

A long-standing weakness in the conduct of U.S. relations with the Saudis over the years has been insensitivity to the psychological factor. Official and unofficial visits of U.S. leaders to Saudi Arabia have all too often undermined Saudi confidence in the strength of the U.S. commitment to Saudi Arabia, particularly in the cases of those officials who have focused on substantive issues during what the Saudis consider ceremonial visits for the purpose of instilling personal mutual trust. Conscious of their role as gracious hosts, the Saudis do not wish to be put on the spot over substantive issues in high-level meetings; they prefer to use such occasions for mutual expressions of goodwill and for publicly announcing agreement over what has already been worked out in advance.

In the long run, U.S.-Saudi relations will stand or fall on personal diplomacy far more than on the terms of negotiation of a given problem or on the scope or nature of programs proffered in the name of cooperation.

Notes

1. Parts of this chapter are based on my article, "U.S.-Saudi Relations: A Foundation of Mutual Needs," in *Arab-American Affairs,* no. 4 (Spring 1983), pp. 12–22.
2. William B. Quandt, *Saudi Arabia's Oil Policy* (Washington, D.C.: Brookings Institution, 1982), p. 129.
3. Ibid., p. 133.
4. Ibid.
5. See, for example, Yossef Bodansky, "Moscow Maneuvers Toward a Takeover in Iran," *Business Week,* August 15, 1983, p. 46.

Abbreviations and Acronyms

AID	Agency for International Development
Aramco	Arabian American Oil Company
ARCO	Atlantic-Richfield
AWACS	airborne warning and control system
Bapco	Bahrain Petroleum Company
BBC	British Broadcasting Corporation
CAGNE	Commerce Action Group on the Near East
Caltex	California Texas Oil Company Ltd.
Casoc	California Arabian Standard Oil Company
CENTCOM	U.S. Central Command
CENTO	Central Treaty Organization
CFIUS	Committee of Foreign Investment in the United States
CIA	Central Intelligence Agency
COE	Corps of Engineers
DISC	domestic international sales corporation
FEA	Federal Energy Administration
FMS	Foreign Military Sales
GAO	General Accounting Office
GCC	Gulf Cooperation Council
IEA	International Energy Agency
I-Hawk	improved Hawk
IMF	International Monetary Fund
IPC	Iraq Petroleum Company
IRS	Internal Revenue Service
MAP	Military Assistance Program

MEDO	Middle East Defense Organization
NBC	National Broadcasting Corporation
OAPEC	Organization of Arab Petroleum Exporting Countries
OFIUS	Office of Foreign Investment in the United States
OPEC	Organization of Petroleum Exporting Countries
OSS	Office of Strategic Services
PDRY	People's Democratic Republic of Yemen
PLO	Palestine Liberation Organization
Polisario	Popular Front for the Liberation of Saquia-el-Hamra and Rio de Oro
PRSY	People's Republic of Southern Yemen
RAMP	Armaments Repair and Maintenance Program
RDF	rapid deployment force
SAC	Strategic Air Command
SAM	surface-to-air missiles
SAMA	Saudi Arabian Monetary Agency
SAMP	Sauri Arabian Mobility Program
SANG	Saudi Arabian National Guard Program
Satco	Saudi Arabian Tanker Company
SNEP	Saudi Arabian Naval Expansion Plan
Socal	Standard Oil Company of California
Socony	Standard Oil Company of New York
TAFT	Training Assistance Field Team
Tapline	Trans-Arabian Pipeline Company
Tapline	the Trans-Arabian pipeline
Texaco	The Texas Company
TIC	Treasury International Capital
TOW	tube-launched optically tracked wire-guided missiles
TPC	Turkish Petroleum Company
TWA	Trans World Airlines
UAE	United Arab Emirates
UAR	United Arab Republic
UN	United Nations
USAF	U.S. Air Force
USGS	U.S. Geological Survey
USMTM	U.S. Military Training Mission

Selected Bibliography

Abed, George. "Arab Oil-Exporters in the World Economy." *American-Arab Affairs,* no. 3 (Winter 1982-1983), pp. 26–40.

Aburdene, Odeh. "Falling Oil Prices and the World Economy." *American-Arab Affairs,* no. 4 (Spring 1983), pp. 46–52.

Adelman, M. A. "Is the Oil Shortage Real? Oil Companies as OPEC Tax Collectors." *Foreign Policy* 9 (Winter 1972-1973), pp. 69–107.

Akins, James E. "The Oil Crisis: This Time the Wolf Is Here." *Foreign Affairs* 51, no. 3 (April 1973), pp. 462–490.

Almana, Mohammed. *Arabia Unified: A Portrait of Ibn Saud.* London: Hutchison Benham, 1980.

Aramco. *Aramco Handbook: Oil and the Middle East.* Dhahran, Saudi Arabia: Arabian American Oil Company, 1968.

Beling, Willard A., ed. *King Faisal and the Modernisation of Saudi Arabia.* London: Croom Helm; and Boulder, Colo.: Westview Press; 1980.

Braibanti, Ralph, and Fouad Abdul-Salam Al-Farsy. "Saudi Arabia: A Developmental Perspective." *Journal of South Asian and Middle Eastern Studies* 1, no. 2 (September 1977), pp. 3–34.

Campbell, John C. "The Middle East: House of Containment Built on Shifting Sands." *Foreign Affairs* 59, no. 4 (1981), pp. 593–628.

Choucri, Nazli. *International Politics of Energy Interdependence.* Lexington, Mass.: Lexington Books, 1976.

Chubin, Shahram. *Security in the Persian Gulf: The Role of Outside Powers.* London: International Institute for Strategic Studies, 1981.

Cleron, Jean Paul. *Saudi Arabia 2000.* London: Croom Helm, 1978.

Cordesman, Anthony H. "After AWACS: Establishing Western Security Throughout Southwest Asia." *Armed Forces Journal* 19, no. 1 (December 1981), pp. 64–68.

———. *The Gulf and the Search for Strategic Stability: Saudi Arabia, the Military Balance in the Gulf, and the Trends in the Arab-Israeli Military Balance.* Boulder, Colo.: Westview Press; and London: Mansell Publishing; 1984.

Cottrell, Alvin J., ed. *The Persian Gulf: A General Survey.* Baltimore: Johns Hopkins University Press, 1980.

Dawisha, Adeed I. *Saudi Arabia's Search for Security.* Adelphi Paper no. 158. London: International Institute for Strategic Studies, winter 1979-1980.

Eddy, William A. *FDR Meets Ibn Saud.* New York: American Friends of the Middle East, 1954.

Eilts, Hermann F. "Security Considerations in the Persian Gulf." *International Security* 5, no. 2 (Fall 1980), pp. 79–113.

Feis, Herbert. *Seen From E.A.: Three International Episodes.* New York: Alfred A. Knopf, 1947.

Ferrell, Robert H., ed. *The Eisenhower Diaries.* New York and London: W. W. Norton, 1981.

Finer, Herman. *Dulles over Suez: The Theory and Practice of His Diplomacy.* Chicago: Quadrangle Books, 1964.

Haig, Alexander M. *Caveat: Realism, Reagan and Foreign Policy.* New York: Macmillan, 1984.

Hayes, Steven D. "Joint Economic Commissions as Instruments of U.S. Foreign Policy in the Middle East." *Middle East Journal* 31, no. 1 (Winter 1977), pp. 16–30.

Helms, Christian Moss. *The Cohesion of Saudi Arabia.* Baltimore: Johns Hopkins University Press, 1981.

Holden, David, and Richard Johns. *The House of Saud.* London: Sidgwick and Jackson, 1981.

Hopwood, Derek, ed. *The Arabian Peninsula: Society and Politics.* London: George Allen & Unwin, 1972.

International Institute for Strategic Studies. *The Middle East and the International System.* Parts 1 and 2. Adelphi Papers nos. 114 and 115. London: International Institute for Strategic Studies, 1975.

Johany, Ali D. *The Myth of the OPEC Cartel: The Role of Saudi Arabia.* New York: John Wiley, 1982.

Kanovsky, Eliyahu. "Saudi Arabia in the Red." *Jerusalem Quarterly,* no. 16 (Summer 1980), pp. 137–144.

Kelly, J. B. *Arabia, the Gulf and the West: A Critical View of the Arabs and Their Oil Policy.* New York: Basic Books, 1980.

Kirk, George. *The Middle East in the War.* New York and London: Oxford University Press, 1953.

Kissinger, Henry A. *For the Record: Selected Statements, 1977–1980.* Boston: Little, Brown, 1979.

______. *White House Years.* Boston: Little, Brown, 1979.

Krapels, Edward N., ed. *Oil and Security.* Adelphi Paper no. 136. London: International Institute for Strategic Studies, 1977.

______. "International Oil Supplies and Stockpiling." In proceedings of a conference held in Hamburg, September 17 and 18, 1981. London: Economist Intelligence Unit, 1982.

Lacey, Robert. *The Kingdom.* London: Hutchinson, 1981.

Lebkicher, Roy, George Rentz, and Max Steinecke, eds. *The Arabia of Ibn Saud.* New York: Russell F. Moore for Aramco, 1952.

______. *Aramco Handbook.* Dhahran, Saudi Arabia: Aramco, 1960.

Long, David E. *Saudi Arabia.* The Washington Papers 4, no. 39. Beverly Hills, Calif., and London: Sage Publications, 1976.

———. *The Persian Gulf: An Introduction to Its Peoples, Politics, and Economics.* Rev. ed. Boulder, Colo.: Westview Press, 1978.

———. *The Hajj Today: A Survey of the Contemporary Makkah Pilgrimage.* Albany: State University of New York Press, 1979.

———. "Saudi Oil Policy." *Wilson Quarterly* 3, (Winter 1979), pp. 83–91.

———. "U.S.-Saudi Relations: A Foundation of Mutual Needs." *American-Arab Affairs,* no. 4 (Spring 1983), pp. 12–22.

Looney, Robert E. *Saudi Arabia's Development Potential.* Lexington, Mass.: Lexington Books, 1982.

Lowenfeld, Andreas F. "Sauce for the Gander . . . The Arab Boycott and United States Political Trade Controls." *Texas International Law Journal* 12, no. 1 (1977), pp. 25–39.

Mallakh, Ragaei El. *OPEC: Twenty Years and Beyond.* Boulder, Colo.: Westview Press, 1982.

———. *Saudi Arabia: Rush to Development.* London: Croom Helm, 1982.

Mallakh, Ragaei El, and Dorothea H. El Mallakh, eds. *Saudi Arabia: Energy, Developmental Planning, and Industrialization.* Lexington, Mass., and Toronto: Lexington Books, 1982.

Miller, Aaron David. *Search for Security: Saudi Arabian Oil and American Foreign Policy, 1939–1949.* Chapel Hill: University of North Carolina Press, 1980.

Nawwab, Ismail I., Peter C. Speers, and Paul F. Hoye, eds. *Aramco and Its World: Arabia and the Middle East.* Dhahran, Saudi Arabia: Arabian American Oil Company, 1980.

Niblock, Tim, ed. *State, Society, and the Economy in Saudi Arabia.* London: Croom Helm, 1982.

Nyrop, Richard F. *Area Handbook for Saudi Arabia.* Foreign Area Studies. Washington, D.C.: American University Press, 1977.

Ochsenwald, William. "Saudi Arabia and the Islamic Revival." *International Journal of Middle East Studies* 13, no. 3 (August 1981), pp. 271–286.

Painter, David Sydney. "The Politics of Oil: Multinational Oil Corporations and United States Foreign Policy, 1941–1954." Ph.D. dissertation. University of North Carolina at Chapel Hill, 1982.

Peck, Malcolm. "Saudi Arabia in United States Foreign Policy to 1958: A Case Study in the Sources and Determinants of American Policy." Ph.D. dissertation. Fletcher School of Law and Diplomacy, 1970.

Philby, H. St. John B. *Arabian Oil Ventures.* Washington, D.C.: Middle East Institute, 1964.

Preece, Richard M. "The Saudi Peace Proposals." Washington, D.C.: Congressional Research Service, Library of Congress, November 24, 1981.

Quandt, William B. *The Rapid Deployment Force.* Cambridge, Mass.: Institute for Foreign Policy Analysis, 1981.

———. *Saudi Arabia in the 1980s: Foreign Policy, Security and Oil.* Washington, D.C.: Brookings Institution, 1981.

———. *Saudi Arabia's Oil Policy: A Staff Paper.* Washington, D.C.: Brookings Institution, 1982.

Rustow, Dankwart. "U.S.-Saudi Relations and the Oil Crisis of the 1980s." *Foreign Affairs* 55, no. 3 (April 1977), pp. 494–516.

Sampson, Anthony. *The Arms Bazaar: From Lebanon to Lockheed.* New York: Viking Press, 1977.

Shaw, John A., and David E. Long. *Saudi Arabian Modernization: The Impact of Change on Stability.* The Washington Papers 10, no. 89. New York: Praeger Publications, 1982.

Stocking, George W. *Middle East Oil: A Study in Political and Economic Controversy.* Nashville, Tenn.: Vanderbilt University Press, 1970.

Stoff, Michael B. *Oil, War, and American Security: The Search for a National Policy on Foreign Oil, 1941–47.* New Haven, Conn.: Yale University Press, 1980.

Turck, Nancy. "The Arab Boycott of Israel." *Foreign Affairs* 55, no. 3 (April 1977), pp. 472–493.

U.S. Arms Control and Disarmament Agency. *World Military Expenditures and Arms Transfers, 1966–1975 and 1969–1978.* Washington, D.C.: Government Printing Office, 1980.

U.S. Congress. House of Representatives. Committee on Foreign Affairs. *Economic and Military Cooperation with Nations in the Middle East.* Hearings before the Committee on Foreign Affairs on H.J. Res. 117 (Eisenhower Doctrine), 85th Cong., 1st sess. Washington, D.C.: Government Printing Office, 1957.

———. *U.S. Interests in, and Policies Toward, the Persian Gulf, 1980.* No. 68-184-0. Washington, D.C.: Government Printing Office, 1980.

———. *Saudi Arabia and the United States: The New Context in an Evolving Special Relationship.* No. 81-494-0. Washington, D.C.: Government Printing Office, 1981.

———. *U.S. Security Interests in the Persian Gulf.* No. 73-354-0. Washington, D.C.: Government Printing Office, 1981.

U.S. Congress, House of Representatives. Committee on Government Operations Subcommittee on Commerce, Consumer and Monetary Affairs. *The Operations of Federal Agencies in Monitoring, Reporting on, and Analyzing Foreign Investments in the United States.* Pt. 2, *OPEC Investment in the United States.* 96th Cong., 1st sess., July 16, 17, 18, and 26, 1979; and pt. 5, *Appendices,* September 19, 20, and 21, 1978; July 16, 17, 18, 26, 30, and 31 and August 1, 1979. Washington, D.C.: Government Printing Office, 1979 and 1980.

———. Subcommittee on Commerce, Consumer, and Monetary Affairs. *Federal Response to OPEC Country Investments in the United States.* Pt. 2, *Investments in Sensitive Sectors of the U.S. Economy: Kuwait Petroleum Corporation Takeover of Santa Fe International Corporation.* 97th Cong., 1st Sess., October 20, 22; November 24; and December 9, 1981; and pt. 3, *Saudi Arabian Influence on the Whittaker Corporation.* 97th Cong., 2d sess., April 6, 1982. Washington, D.C.: Government Printing Office, 1982.

U.S. Congress. Joint Economic Committee. *The Political Economy of the Middle East, 1973–78.* No. 51-623-0. Washington, D.C.: Government Printing Office, 1980.

U.S. Congress. Library of Congress. "The Persian Gulf: Are We Committed?" Washington, D.C., 1981.

U.S. Congress. Library of Congress. Congressional Research Service. *Project Interdependence: U.S. and World Energy Outlook Through 1990.* No. 95-31. Washington, D.C.: Government Printing Office, 1977.

———. "Saudi Arabia and the United States: The New Context in an Evolving Special Relationship." Washington, D.C.: Government Printing Office, August 1981.

U.S. Congress. Senate. *Petroleum Arrangements with Saudi Arabia.* Hearings before a Special Committee Investigating the National Defense Program, 80th Cong., 1st sess. Washington, D.C.: Government Printing Office, 1948.

———. *The President's Proposal on the Middle East* (Eisenhower Doctrine). Hearings before the Committee on Foreign Relations and the Committee on Armed Services on S.J. and H.J. 117. Pt. 2. Washington, D.C.: Government Printing Office, 1957.

———. *Multinational Corporations and United States Foreign Policy; Hearings Before the Subcommittee on Multinational Corporations of the Committee on Foreign Relations.* Pt. 6; pts. 7 and 8, 93rd Cong., 2d sess., 1975; pt. 9; pt. 12, 94th Cong., lst sess., 1975; pt. 14, 94th Cong., 2d sess., 1976. Washington, D.C.: Government Printing Office, 1975 and 1976.

U.S. Congress. Senate. Committee on Energy and Natural Resources. *Geopolitics of Oil.* No. 96-119. Washington, D.C.: Government Printing Office, 1980.

U.S. Congress. Senate. Select Committee on Small Business. *The International Petroleum Cartel.* Washington, D.C.: Government Printing Office, 1952.

U.S. Department of Commerce. International Trade Administration. Office of Antiboycott Compliance. "Restrictive Trade Practices or Boycotts Including Enforcement in Administrative Proceedings." Reprinted from *Export Administrative Regulations.* Washington, D.C.: Government Printing Office, 1983.

U.S. Department of Defense. Defense Security Assistance Agency Foreign Sales. *Foreign Military Construction Sales and Military Assistance Facts as of September 1982.* Washington, D.C.: Government Printing Office, 1983.

U.S. Department of State. *Bulletin.* Selected copies.

———. *Foreign Relations of the United States* (*FRUS*). Washington, D.C.: Government Printing Office, selected volumes and years.

———. *Treaties and Other International Acts Series* (*TIAS*). Washington, D.C.: Government Printing Office, selected years.

———. *United States Treaties* (*UST*). Washington, D.C.: Government Printing Office, selected years.

U.S. Department of State. Office of the Historian. "The Evolution of OPEC, 1959–1983." Historical Research Project no. 1349.

U.S. Federal Energy Administration. "Project Independence: A Summary." Washington, D.C.: Government Printing Office, November 1974.

U.S. Federal Energy Administration. Office of Economic Impact. "The Economic Impact of the Oil Embargo on the American Economy." Washington, D.C.: Federal Energy Administration, August 8, 1974.

U.S. General Accounting Office. *The U.S.–Saudi Arabian Joint Commission on Economic Cooperation.* Report by the comptroller of the United States, March 22, 1979. ID-79-7. Washington, D.C.: Government Printing Office, 1979.

______. *Reimbursement of Federal Employees' Salaries and Benefits by Saudi Arabia.* Report to the chairman, Subcommittee on Commerce, Consumer, and Monetary Affairs, Committee on Government Operations, House of Representatives, October 21, 1982. GAO/ID-83-4. Washington, D.C.: General Accounting Office, 1982.

______. *Status of U.S.–Saudi Arabian Joint Commission on Economic Cooperation.* Report by the comptroller general of the United States to the chairman, Subcommittee on Europe and the Middle East, Committee on Foreign Affairs, House of Representatives, May 26, 1983. GAO/ID-83-32. Washington, D.C.: General Accounting Office, 1983.

Walpole, Norman C., et al. *Area Handbook for Saudi Arabia.* American University Foreign Area Studies series. Washington, D.C.: Government Printing Office, 1971.

Weisberg, Richard Chadbourn. *The Politics of Crude Oil Pricing in the Middle East, 1970–1975: A Study in International Bargaining.* Research Series no. 31. Berkeley: Institute of International Studies, University of California, 1977.

Wells, Donald A. *Saudi Arabian Development Strategy.* Washington, D.C.: American Enterprise Institute, 1976.

Young, Arthur N. "Economic Review: Saudi Arabian Currency and Finance." Pt. 1. *Middle East Journal* 7, no. 3 (1953), pp. 361–380. Pt. 2, *Middle East Journal* 7, no. 4 (1953), pp. 539–556.

______. *Saudi Arabia: The Making of a Financial Giant.* New York: New York University Press, 1983.

Index